EYEWITNESS

American Originals from the National Archives

With a Foreword by Allen Weinstein, Archivist of the United States

by

Stacey Bredhoff

Philip Wilson Publishers in collaboration with
The Foundation for the National Archives, Washington, DC

This book is based on the exhibition "Eyewitness—American Originals from the National Archives," presented at the National Archives from June 23, 2006, through January 1, 2007. A traveling version of "Eyewitness" is planned to visit six sites on a nationwide tour over the subsequent two and a half years.

In the interest of the long-term preservation of the documents, some of the eyewitness accounts will be rotated throughout the course of the exhibit tour. Some of the documents presented in the book may not be displayed at all venues; similarly, not all accounts seen at the venues are presented in this book.

The quotes from the eyewitness accounts retain the original spelling and punctuation, except where indicated by the use of brackets.

The exhibition, "Eyewitness," was created by the National Archives and Records Administration, Washington, DC, and the Foundation for the National Archives.

First published in 2006 by
Philip Wilson Publishers
109 Drysdale Street
The Timber Yard
London N1 6ND

in collaboration with
The Foundation for the National Archives
700 Pennsylvania Avenue, NW
Washington, DC 20408-0001

Hardback trade edition distributed throughout the world (excluding north America) by
I.B. Tauris & Co. Ltd
6 Salem Road, London W2 4BU
Distributed in North America by
Palgrave Macmillan, A division of St Martin's Press
175 Fifth Avenue
New York, NY 10010

Above, third image from left: Photograph by Mark Fiennes, 1997, Courtesy of The Royal Collection © 2006, Her Majesty Queen Elizabeth II

These eyewitness accounts are drawn from the nationwide holdings of the National Archives, including the Presidential libraries and regional archives.

Printed in China

Contents

Foreword

From the Archivist of the United States

Few aspects of American history are as compelling as an eyewitness account of an event that changed the course of history or was a defining moment in the story of our democracy.

The immediacy conveyed by freshly written words of people who participated in or observed these events firsthand is difficult to replicate, even by the most gifted of historians, since eyewitness accounts can often capture the atmosphere and mood, tension and passion, joy or sorrow of both triumphant and tragic events.

Picture George Washington in Cambridge, Massachusetts, as commander in chief of the American Revolutionary forces in December 1775. He has heard that the British may be deliberately spreading smallpox, an early act of bioterrorism (if true). Washington made his concerns clear in a letter to John Hancock, President of the Continental Congress, meeting in Philadelphia.

Imagine Laura Ingalls Wilder—author of *Little House on the Prairie* and other popular children's books—as a wife and mother, traveling with her family from South Dakota to Missouri in search of a better life. Her impressions and recollections of the trip were carefully chronicled in one of her journals.

Sit with George H.W. Bush, then Chairman of the Republican National Committee, in the White House East Room as Richard M. Nixon bids farewell to the Cabinet and White House staff on his last day as President, August 9, 1974. Bush's impressions of the first President to resign from office are recorded in his diary for that day.

In this volume, *Eyewitness—American Originals from the National Archives*, you can read the words of Washington, Wilder, and Bush. They

Earthrise, photograph by Bill Anders, 1968
Records of the U.S. Information Agency [306-PSD-68-4049c]

will tell you of the struggle to achieve an unlikely victory in the War for Independence, of what it was like to travel long distances by covered wagon, and of how one observer felt watching a President take his emotional leave from public office.

Following our earlier critically acclaimed exhibit, "American Originals: Treasures from the National Archives," which ran for five years in the National Archives Building in Washington before touring the country, we assembled once more a selection of documents that provide details and insights into the story of America. The result was an exhibit, "Eyewitness—American Originals from the National Archives," which opened in 2006 in the Lawrence F. O'Brien Gallery at the National Archives Building. Here, in the pages of this book, you will find that exhibit.

For "Eyewitness," we reached into the National Archives' vast holdings—from facilities in Washington, DC, from regional archives around the country, and from some of our Presidential libraries—for accounts by individuals who were present at historic and defining events representing the broad sweep of American history.

Look for Adams, Jefferson, and Washington from the Revolutionary era, their letters describing some of the historic moments and forgotten details of the nation's fight for independence. There are also the voices of a fugitive slave from 1862 and, a century later, a civil rights leader continuing the struggle for equal rights. There are witnesses to triumphs and tragedies, war and peace, journeys across America, and those into space.

In the pages that follow we reproduce many of the primary documents containing these eyewitness accounts, so you can read the words as they were written or spoken by the eyewitnesses themselves—accounts recorded in letters and diaries and on audio or videotape.

These documents represent only a tiny fraction of the records in the National Archives, the nation's record keeper. The National Archives' mission is to provide ready access to essential evidence of the rights of our citizens, the actions of our government, and our national experience. Our mission includes the role of civic educator—to inform Americans young and old of their nation's history through the primary documents that are the foundation of that history.

These records are available at National Archives facilities nationwide, and many of them are available online at *Archives.gov*, where you can also find a version of the "Eyewitness" exhibit.

For this exhibit and this book, we are grateful for generous support from both the Foundation for the National Archives and the National Archives Trust Fund Board.

ALLEN WEINSTEIN
Archivist of the United States

Introduction

Out of the stacks and vaults of the National Archives comes this selection of original, firsthand accounts. They are vivid and intensely personal, transporting us to a deeper understanding of the events described.

Thomas Jefferson, as U.S. Minister to France, was in Paris on July 14, 1789, and reported some of the earliest bloodletting of the French Revolution.

President Lincoln's family physician was at the President's bedside after he was shot at Ford's Theater and later testified to Lincoln's "vital tenacity" as he clung to life through the night of April 14, 1865.

And the crew of the *Apollo 8* spacecraft, in 1968, traveled farther from Earth than anyone ever had and saw their home planet as no one had seen it before: a miracle of color and life suspended in space— shimmering, delicate, and impossibly distant.

These accounts and others add a human dimension to the textbook version of history; the who, what, and where of an event give way to the mystery of a human interaction.

In 1785, after the War for Independence, John Adams was appointed the first U.S. Minister Plenipotentiary to Britain. The American victory in the War for Independence had transformed the King's rebellious colonies into a sovereign nation, and one of its leading "rebels," John Adams, into a statesman. When Adams presented his credentials to King George III at St. James Palace, on June 1, 1785, it was a milestone in international relations and diplomatic history. But a letter from Adams to the U.S. Secretary of State, dated June 2, 1785, reveals the human side of the encounter, as the King, having suffered a bitter defeat at the hands of the Americans, accepted his former subject as a diplomat. Adams's letter recounts the interview almost verbatim.

Opposite: "Young Driver in Mine. Has been driving one year. 7 A.M. to 5:30 P.M daily Brown Mine, Brown W. VA.," photograph and caption by Lewis Hine, 1908. *National Archives, Records of the Children's Bureau [102-LH-136]*

Some of the eyewitnesses have names that are not well known to history. There is John Boston, who, during the Civil War, fled slavery and joined a New York regiment in Upton, Virginia. On January 12, 1862, he wrote to his wife to tell her that he had reached freedom, his joy tempered by the knowledge that he might never see his family again.

Not all of the accounts were handed down in written form. One of the most famous broadcasts in the history of radio journalism—Herb Morrison's 1937 report of the explosion and crash of the *Hindenburg* airship—is preserved at the National Archives. Listeners hear the reporter struggle for composure as a scene of fiery death unfolds before his eyes.

Lewis Hine's eyewitness accounts took the form of photographs. As an investigative photographer with the National Child Labor Committee, he documented children working in coal mines, factories, fields, and street trades. The cover of this book features a young miner whom Hine encountered in West Virginia. Hine's photographs are unflinching, accompanied by his own captions that are sparely written, but filled with facts. Young children with world-weary faces stare out of these photographs, confronting viewers with the truth of child labor in early twentieth-century America.

Lady Bird Johnson left an audio diary entry describing the tragic events of November 22, 1963. She was with her husband, Vice President Lyndon Johnson, riding in the motorcade in Dallas, Texas, when President John F. Kennedy was shot. She recounts how she heard the shots, how the motorcade sped to Parkland Hospital, and how she later found Jacqueline Kennedy, the President's wife, waiting in a hospital corridor as the doctors treated her husband: "She was quite alone. I don't think I ever saw anyone so much alone in my life," Mrs. Johnson recalled.

The accounts in "Eyewitness" are tremendously varied. There are stunning stories of adventure and grisly tales of war. They come to us from people with unique perches and vantage points. Some are told in the heat of the moment, as an event is unfolding; others through a haze of memory and time. Filled with surprising details, they have the ring of truth.

The instinct to tell what we have seen is as old as humanity. Lady Bird Johnson, the former First Lady, said that she recorded the things she saw because she found her experience "too great a thing to have alone." Like-minded Americans from every generation have handed down their stories in untold numbers. Millions of them are preserved in the stacks of the National Archives, waiting to be shared. Within them lie embedded messages that enlighten us on what has gone before, and strengthen us for what may lie ahead.

STACEY BREDHOFF
Curator of "Eyewitness"

Lady Bird Johnson working on her diary in the second floor bedroom of the White House, photograph by Robert Knudsen, November 15, 1968

National Archives, Lyndon Baines Johnson Library and Museum, Austin, Texas

[NLLBJ-D2440-7a]

"*Nothing can be believed or has from an eye*

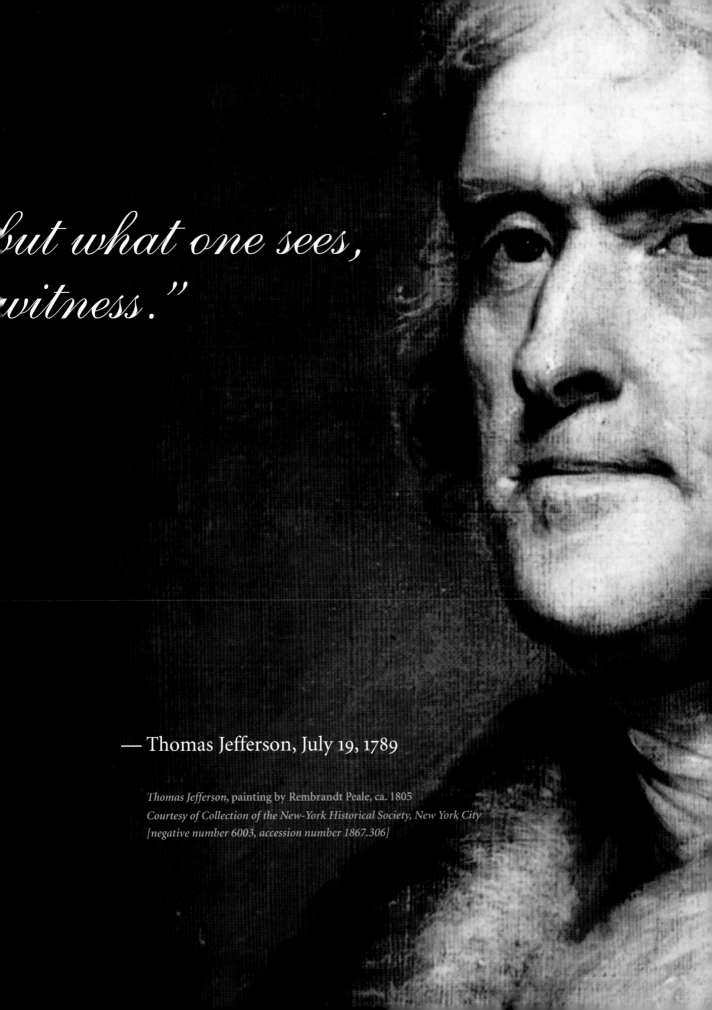

but what one sees,

witness."

— Thomas Jefferson, July 19, 1789

Thomas Jefferson, painting by Rembrandt Peale, ca. 1805
Courtesy of Collection of the New-York Historical Society, New York City
[negative number 6003, accession number 1867.306]

Storming of the Bastille, July 14th, 1789, **painting, unattributed, eighteenth century**
The Bastille loomed large in the French imagination as a mysterious, medieval, dark dungeon of a place where vast numbers of people who had displeased the King would disappear to lead a tortured existence. In fact, by the time of Louis XVI, living conditions inside the Bastille were not at all dire; food was adequate, and prisoners were free to bring in many of their own possessions. On July 14, 1789, this towering symbol of royal oppression held only seven prisoners: two who were mentally ill, four forgers, and one person who had been incarcerated for incest. *Courtesy of Réunion des Musées Nationaux/Art Resource, NY*

❧ Thomas Jefferson

Onset of the French Revolution, 1789

"Nothing can be believed but what one sees, or has from an eye witness."
— Thomas Jefferson, July 19, 1789

Appointed U.S. Minister to France in 1785, Thomas Jefferson was the American Government's man on the ground in Paris in July 1789 when the French people rose up against their rulers and the first blood was shed in the opening days of the French Revolution. Author of the Declaration of Independence whose immortal words had come to define the spirit of the Revolution in America, Jefferson followed closely and with great interest the events of the unfolding Revolution in France.

In 1789, when King Louis XVI summoned the States General, an assembly of nobles, clergy, and citizens that had not convened since 1614, to address a huge financial crisis, Jefferson commuted daily from his lavish house on the outskirts of the city to Versailles to observe the meetings being held there. And in July, when the streets of Paris descended into lawlessness, chaos, and violence, Jefferson and his secretary, William Short, roamed the streets to learn firsthand what was happening.

The storming of the Bastille, the public beheading of its director, a dramatic appearance of the King—these monumental events, clouded by the chaos and uncertainty of the moment—are all told in the calm, clear voice of America's Thomas Jefferson.

Thomas Jefferson, pencil on paper, unattributed, eighteenth century
Courtesy of The Maryland Historical Society, Baltimore, Maryland

"[At the Bastille] They took all the arms, discharged the prisoners & such of the garrison as were not killed in the first moment of fury, carried the Governor & Lieutenant governor to the Greve (the place of public execution) cut off their heads & sent them through the city in triumph to the Palais royal."
—From Thomas Jefferson's letter to John Jay

whom he received them. De Corney advised the people then to retire, retired himself & the people took possession of the arms. It was remarkeable that not only the Invalids themselves made no op--position, but that a body of 5000 foreign troops, encamped within 400. yards, never stirred. Monsieur de Corny and five others were then sent to ask arms of Monsieur de Launai, Governor of the Bastille. They found a great collection of people already before the place, & they immediately planted a flag of truce, which was answered by a like flag hoisted on the parapet. The deputation prevailed on the people to fall back a little, advanced themselves to make their demand of the Governor, & in that instant a discharge from the Bastille killed 4. people of those nearest to the deputies. The deputies retired, the people rushed against the place, and almost in an instant were in possession of a fortification, defended by 100 men, of infinite strength, which in other times had stood several regu--lar sieges & had never been taken. how they got in, has as yet been impossible to discover. those, who pretend to have been of the party tell so many different stories as to destroy the credit of them all. They took all the arms, discharged the prisoners & such of the garrison as were not killed in the first moment of fury, carried the Governor & Lieutenant governor to the Greve (the place of public execution) cut off their heads, & sent them through the city, in triumph to the Palais royal. About the same instant, a treache--rous

Letter from Thomas Jefferson, U.S. Minister to France, to John Jay, Secretary of Foreign Affairs, July 19, 1789, reporting on the events in Paris, selected page
This portion of Jefferson's twelve-page letter—written entirely in his own hand—recounts how a mob seeking to arm themselves, stormed the Bastille (the four-teenth-century fortress used as a prison), took the stash of arms, freed the prison-ers, and seized the "Governor" of the Bastille who was then killed and beheaded in the city streets.

A later portion of the letter recounts the panic at the King's court at Versailles resulting from false reports that a mob of 150,000 was on their way to "massacre the Royal family, the court, the ministers and all connected with them." *National Archives, Records of the Continental and Confederation Congresses and the Constitutional Convention*

Confrontations for Justice

✏ John Lewis

March from Selma to Montgomery, "Bloody Sunday," 1965

" I was hit with a billy club, and I saw the State Trooper that hit me . . . I was hit twice, once when I was lying down and was attempting to get up . . ."

–John Lewis, describing the March 7, 1965, attack on demonstrators
marching from Selma to Montgomery for voting rights

In 1965, at the height of the modern civil rights movement, activists organized a march for voting rights, from Selma, Alabama, to Montgomery, the state capital. On March 7, some 600 people assembled at a downtown church, knelt briefly in prayer, and began walking silently, two-by-two through the city streets. With Hosea Williams of the Southern Christian Leadership Conference (SCLC) leading the demonstration, and John Lewis, Chairman of the Student Nonviolent Coordinating Committee (SNCC), at his side, the marchers were stopped as they were leaving Selma, at the end of the Edmund Pettus Bridge, by some 150 Alabama state troopers, sheriff's deputies, and possemen, who ordered the demonstrators to disperse. One minute and five seconds after a two-minute warning was announced, the troops advanced, wielding clubs, bullwhips, and tear gas. John Lewis, who suffered a skull fracture, was one of fifty-eight people treated for injuries at the local hospital. The day is remembered in history as "Bloody Sunday."

Less than one week later, Lewis recounted the attack on the marchers during a Federal hearing at which the demonstrators sought protection for a full-scale march to Montgomery. A transcript of his testimony is presented in the following pages.

John Lewis (left) and Hosea Williams, July 26, 1965
Six months after "Bloody Sunday," President Lyndon B. Johnson signed into law the Voting Rights Act. One of the pens used by the President hangs framed today in the living room of Representative John Lewis, Fifth U.S. Congressional District of Georgia. He has been elected to that office nine times. *© Bettman/ CORBIS*

"Two Minute Warning," photograph by Spider Martin, March 7, 1965
© 1965 Spider Martin/The Spider Martin Civil Rights Collection.

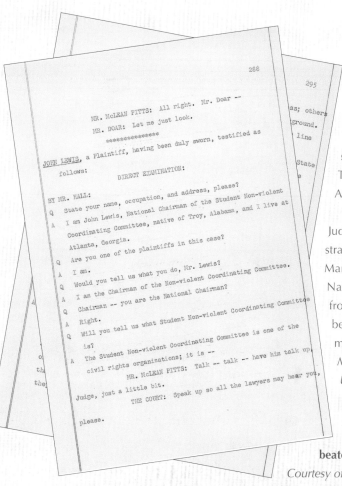

288

MR. McLEAN PITTS: All right. Mr. Doar --

MR. DOAR: Let me just look.

****

JOHN LEWIS, a Plaintiff, having been duly sworn, testified as follows:

DIRECT EXAMINATION:

BY MR. HALL:

Q   State your name, occupation, and address, please?

A   I am John Lewis, National Chairman of the Student Non-violent Coordinating Committee, native of Troy, Alabama, and I live at Atlanta, Georgia.

Q   Are you one of the plaintiffs in this case?

A   I am.

Q   Would you tell us what you do, Mr. Lewis?

A   I am the Chairman of the Non-violent Coordinating Committee.

Q   Chairman -- you are the National Chairman?

A   Right.

Q   Will you tell us what Student Non-violent Coordinating Committee is?

A   The Student Non-violent Coordinating Committee is one of the civil rights organisations; it is --

MR. McLEAN PITTS: Talk -- talk -- have him talk up, Judge, just a little bit.

THE COURT: Speak up so all the lawyers may hear you, please.

295

ss; others
ground.
line

State
e

Testimony of John Lewis from a hearing resulting from the March 7, 1965, march from Selma to Montgomery in support of voting rights, selected pages

These pages show the questions posed by Attorney Hall and John Lewis's responses.

At the end of the hearing, on March 17, Judge Frank Johnson, Jr., ruled that the demonstrators had a constitutional right to march; on March 21, under the protection of a Federalized National Guard, 3,200 demonstrators set out from Selma in a mass demonstration that became a turning point in the civil rights movement. *National Archives—Southeast Region, Morrow, Georgia, Records of District Courts of United States*

Below: John Lewis (in the foreground) being beaten by state troopers, March 7, 1965

Courtesy of AP Images

Lewis: . . . a State Trooper made announcement on a bullhorn or megaphone, and he said, "This march will not continue."

Hall: What happened then; did the line stop?

Lewis: The line stopped at that time.

Hall: You stopped still?

Lewis: Yes, sir.

Hall: You didn't advance any further?

Lewis: We stopped right then.

Hall: Then what happened?

Lewis: He said, "I am Major Cloud, and this is an unlawful assembly. This demonstration will not continue. You have been banned by the Governor. I am going to order you to disperse."

Hall: What did you then do?

Lewis: Mr. Williams said, "Mr. Major, I would like to have a word, can we have a word?" And he said, "No, I will give you two minutes to leave." And again Mr. Williams said, "Can I have a word?" He said, "There will be no word." And about a minute or more Major Cloud ordered the Troopers to advance, and at that time the State Troopers took their position, I guess, and they moved forward with their clubs up over their—near their shoulder, the top part of the body; they came rushing in, knocking us down and pushing us.

Hall: And were you hit at that time?

Lewis: At that time I was hit and knocked down.

Hall: Where were you hit?

Lewis: I was hit on my head right here.

Hall: What were you hit with?

Lewis: I was hit with a billy club, and I saw the State Trooper that hit me.

Hall: How many times were you hit?

Lewis: I was hit twice, once when I was lying down and was attempting to get up.

Hall: Do we understand you to say were hit . . . and then attempted to get up and were hit—and was hit again.

Lewis: Right.

—From John Lewis's testimony

❧ Mr. Beverly Jones

Susan B. Anthony at the Voting Polls, 1872

" She said she was a citizen of the U.S. & demanded her right to be registered. . ."

—Mr. Beverly W. Jones, who registered Susan B. Anthony to vote in the election of 1872

Susan B. Anthony, 1870
Courtesy of the Nebraska State Historical Society Photographic Collections, Lincoln, Nebraska

***Right:* United States Courthouse at Canandaigua, New York, not dated**
Susan B. Anthony's trial took place inside this building. *From the Collections of the Ontario County Historical Society, Canandaigua, NY*

Susan B. Anthony devoted more than fifty years of her life to the cause of woman suffrage. After casting her ballot in the 1872 Presidential election in her hometown of Rochester, New York, she was arrested, indicted, tried, and convicted for voting illegally. At her two-day trial in June 1873, which she later described as "the greatest judicial outrage history has ever recorded," she was convicted and sentenced to pay a fine of $100 and court costs.

After Anthony's arrest, which occurred two weeks after the November 5 election, there was a hearing to determine if she had, in fact, broken the law. The three young men who registered her as a voter on November 1, 1872, and accepted her ballot at the polls on Election Day were interviewed at the hearing.

> " . . . I made the remark that I didn't think we could register her name. She asked me upon what grounds. I told her that the constitution of the State of New York only gave the right of franchise to male citizens. She asked me if I was acquainted with the 14th amendment to the constitution of the U.S. I told her I was. She wanted to know if under that she was a citizen and had a right to vote. At this time, Mr. Warner [the Supervisor of Elections] said, 'young man, how are you going to get around that. I think you will have to register their names'—or something to that effect."

—From Beverly Jones's testimony

Testimony of Mr. Beverly W. Jones, an election official in Rochester, New York, who was confronted by Susan B. Anthony on November 1, 1872, selected pages

In this portion of Jones's testimony, he relates his encounter with Susan B. Anthony on November 1, 1872, when she entered a barbershop that had been set up as an office of voter registration and demanded that her name be added to the list of voters. *National Archives–Northeast Region (New York City), Records of District Courts of the United States*

❧ Gen. George Washington

A Threat of Bioterrorism, 1775

Bioterrorism was among the many concerns that occupied Gen. George Washington in the winter of 1775, six months after taking command of the ragtag American forces in Cambridge, Massachusetts. The years of the American Revolution coincided nearly perfectly with a smallpox epidemic that spanned the North American continent claiming more than 130,000 lives from 1775 to 1782. And Washington had reason to believe that the British were waging germ warfare by deliberately infecting American troops with the highly contagious and deadly smallpox virus.

Washington knew firsthand the misery of the disease having survived a smallpox infection years earlier; he was well aware that a smallpox epidemic would ravage his fledgling armies. It is impossible to know with certainty whether the British practiced germ warfare against the Americans or not. However, a series of letters from Washington to Congress written in December 1775 reveal that the threat of biological warfare was sufficiently real in his mind to merit mention in his official reports. First, his fears were based on a report that he heard and then fuelled by what he saw with his own eyes.

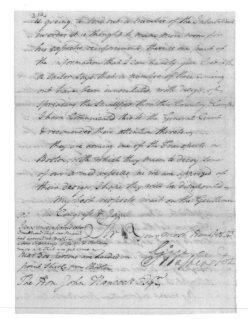

Letter from Gen. George Washington to John Hancock, President of Congress, regarding an alleged plot of the British to spread smallpox among the American troops, December 4, 1775, signature page

Before closing a lengthy letter to Congress reporting on a variety of topics, Washington passed along information that he had heard from a sailor: that British Gen. William Howe was sending people out from Boston who had been deliberately infected with smallpox so that they might pass on the disease to the Americans surrounding the city. After seeing an increased number of cases in people coming out of Boston, Washington came to believe that smallpox was indeed "a weapon of Defence they Are useing against us." *National Archives, Records of the Continental and Confederation Congresses and the Constitutional Convention*

"By recent information from Boston, Genl Howe is goeing to Send out a number of the Inhabitants in order it is thought to make more room for his expected reinforcements, there is one part of the information that I Can hardly give Credit to. A Sailor Says that a number of these Comeing out have been innoculated, with design of Spreading the Smallpox thro' this Country & Camp. I have Communicated this to the General Court & recommended their attention thereto."

—From George Washington's letter to Congress

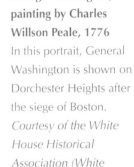

George Washington, painting by Charles Willson Peale, 1776
In this portrait, General Washington is shown on Dorchester Heights after the siege of Boston. *Courtesy of the White House Historical Association (White House Collection), Washington, DC*

∻ Herb Morrison

Hindenburg Disaster, 1937

"Oh, the humanity, and all the passengers screaming around here!"

—Radio reporter Herb Morrison describing the
explosion and crash of the *Hindenburg*, May 6, 1937

Herb Morrison, photo-graph appeared in ***Stand By*** **magazine, published by WLS, May 15, 1937**
Courtesy of Library of American Broadcasting, University of Maryland, College Park, Maryland

One of the most famous broadcasts in the history of radio journalism is Herb Morrison's 1937 eyewitness report of the explosion and crash of the German passenger airship, *Hindenburg*. On May 6, 1937, while preparing to land at the Lakehurst Naval Air Station in New Jersey, the *Hindenburg* burst into flames and crashed to the ground, killing thirty-five of the ninety-seven people on board and one member of the ground crew.

Chicago radio station WLS had sent reporter Herb Morrison and sound engineer Charles Nehlsen to record the landing which was being celebrated as the first anniversary of the inauguration of transatlantic passenger service and the opening of the 1937 season. Morrison's professional demeanor as he described the landing gave way to an emotional outburst of exclamations after the *Hindenburg* caught fire. Shaken and horrified, Morrison continued to record, struggling to compose himself as a hellish scene of fiery death unfolded before his eyes.

From the Radio Report on the *Hindenburg*
Disaster, May 6, 1937

"It's fire and it's crashing! . . . This is the worst of the worst catastrophes in the world! Oh, it's crashing . . . oh, four or five hundred feet into the sky, and it's a terrific crash, ladies and gentlemen. There's smoke, and there's flames, now, and the frame is crashing to the ground, not quite to the mooring mast. Oh, the humanity, and all the passengers screaming around here!

. . . I can't talk, ladies and gentlemen. Honest, it's just laying there, a mass of smoking wreckage, and everybody can hardly breathe and talk . . . Honest, I can hardly breathe. I'm going to step inside where I cannot see it. . . ."

Later in the broadcast, as he learned that there were survivors, he said, "I hope that it isn't as bad as I made it sound at the very beginning."

Years later, Morrison recalled that he yelled "Oh, the humanity," because he thought everyone on board had died; in fact, sixty-two of the people on board survived.

Portions of the broadcast were aired for the first time the following day. The original disks on which the recording were made were donated to the National Archives by WLS, Chicago's Prairie Farmer radio station, and are among the holdings of the Special Media Archives—Donated Materials.

Hindenburg Explosion, May 6, 1937
© *Bettman/CORBIS*

❧ Marie Adams

Internment of American Civilians in the Philippines, 1945

"We were hungry; we were starved. When I went to bed at night, I felt just on the verge of screaming. I ached to the ends of my fingers and toes, with the most horrible ache that I have ever experienced."

—Marie Adams, American Red Cross worker, describing her final
days at a civilian prison camp in Japanese-occupied Philippines, 1945

The invasion of the Philippines came hours after the Japanese attack on Pearl Harbor on December 7, 1941. Thousands of American civilians living in the Philippines were captured and held in captivity by the Japanese until the end of World War II. As the war progressed, the internees found themselves living a nightmare of steadily deteriorating conditions inside the camps—struggling for food and other necessities of life over a three-year period.

Santo Tomas University, in downtown Manila, was converted to an internment camp that held more than 4,000 civilians. Among them was Marie Adams, a Red Cross worker, approximately fifty years old, who was held there from May 1942 until the camp was liberated in February 1945. Throughout her confinement, she worked in the compound's hospital, adapting to the increasing medical needs of the camp's population, even as her own physical condition declined. Four months after the camp was liberated, she wrote a report describing the dire conditions in the camp and how she calmly calculated how to ensure the survival of the greatest number of the internees, as well as her own.

this way that no official list of prisoners in the military camps in the Philippines had ever been submitted by the Japanese to the United States Government. When we read that each week a food kit was being distributed to prisoners held in Europe, I think our morale hit an all-time low. We had known that we were isolated from the world, but the fact was truly driven home to us by that information more than anything else. We felt that we were indeed the "lost tribes of the Philippines"—no contact with home, no contact with the Red Cross, no contact with the outside at all, and none to be expected. People became very nervous and irritable that year. The mail situation was a contributing factor. Some in the camp received none at all. I received my first letter, then eighteen months old, in March, 1944. Between then and November, 1944, I received altogether sixty-eight letters, none of which was younger than a year. My family received my first letter two weeks before I was liberated. Beginning in February, 1944, we were each allowed to send a postal card a month. I sent eleven. So far my family has received the ones I wrote in March and May of last year and just last week, the one I wrote in July.

In my May card, which they received just before I was liberated, I asked them to send me milk, meat, sugar, butter, chocolate, soap, and various toiletries. I thought that that might convey the message that we had nothing to go on. However, just after that, in June, the Japs forbid us to give any further information about what we needed or wanted.

Among the minor irritants toward the last was the fact that we had to bow to every Jap we met. That seemed to get on people's nerves more than any other single thing. It didn't particularly disturb me, because I had had to do it at the military camp where I had been interned previously. During the last few months there was a tension among the internees that is almost indescribable. Irritability is one of the first symptoms of starvation, and certainly that symptom was marked among us. We were all cross, irritable, and edgy; we argued about things that were utterly insignificant. We were ready to claw each other's eyes out—over nothing at all. We were hungry; we were starved. When I went to bed at night, I felt just on the verge of screaming. I ached to the ends of my fingers and toes, with the most horrible ache that I have ever experienced. We were so thoroughly depleted that frequently I would sit on my bed and stare at the sink in the corner of the room, wondering whether it was worth while to make the effort to get up and go over to it to wash my hands, or whether it wouldn't be better to wait until lunch-time to do it, because it would save that much energy.

Everyone was stooped with fatigue. Many had horrible skin conditions. Tropical ulcers and boils were developing everywhere, and infections were on the increase. To aggravate the situation, there

-26-

Marie Adams's report on conditions at the Santo Tomas internment camp, June 7, 1945, selected page
In this report, Adams notes a drastic decline in the living conditions beginning in February 1944, when the administration of the camp shifted from Japanese civilian to Japanese military authority. From that point forward, she chronicles a desperate effort on the part of the internees to stave off starvation long enough to be rescued.

In the final pages of this report, Miss Adams concluded that, had the internees not been rescued in early February 1945, they would have died within three to four weeks. Based on her own level of activity—the work she was doing to care for others—she calculated that she would have been dead in four to five days. She weighed ninety-five pounds at the time the camp was liberated. *National Archives, Records of the Office of the Surgeon General (Army)*

202141

Shanties were built in a courtyard at Santo Tomas to help ease the overcrowding in the buildings, 1945
National Archives, Records of the Office of the Chief Signal Officer [111-SC-202141]

Opposite page: **Photostats of Marie Adams, included in her official report, submitted 1945**
These photostats show how she looked in 1941, prior to her departure for the Philippines, and in 1945, at the time of her liberation.

Miss Adams was awarded the Bronze Star Medal "for meritorious achievement while in the hands of the enemy in caring for the sick and wounded." *National Archives, Records of the Office of the Surgeon General (Army)*

"Irritability is one of the first symptoms of starvation, and certainly that symptom was marked among us. We were all cross, irritable, and edgy; we argued about things that were utterly insignificant. We were ready to claw each other's eyes out—over nothing at all. We were hungry; we were starved. When I went to bed at night, I felt just on the verge of screaming. I ached to the ends of my fingers and toes, with the most horrible ache that I have ever experienced. We were so thoroughly depleted that frequently I would sit on my bed and stare at the sink in the corner of the room, wondering whether it was worth while to make the effort to get up and go over to it to wash my hands, or whether it wouldn't be better to wait until lunch-time to do it, because it would save that much energy. . . .

If we had not been liberated when we were, I believe that the majority of the internees would have been dead within three or four weeks. Considering the amount of work that I was doing and the amount of food that I was eating, I think that I would probably have lived only another four or five days. . . ."

—From Marie Adams's report

❧ Pfc. Harold Porter

Atrocities at Dachau Concentration Camp, 1945

"Certainly, what I have seen in the past few days will affect my personality for the rest of my life. . . . It is easy to read about atrocities, but they must be seen before they can be believed."

—Pfc. Harold Porter, writing to his parents from Dachau concentration camp, May 7, 1945

During the twelve years of the Third Reich (1933–45), the Nazi regime and its dreaded SS established and operated a system of concentration camps to imprison those groups of people whom its leaders perceived to represent a "racial" or political threat to Nazi authority. Nazi leaders identified the European Jews as the priority enemy of Germany and sought to physically annihilate them. The Germans and their Axis partners murdered approximately six million Jews, as well as millions of other innocent men, women, and children during the era of the Holocaust.

Dachau was the first concentration camp established under the authority of the SS. More than 28,000 people died at Dachau between 1940 and 1945, but the total number of deaths at the camp is not known. By April 1945 the water, sewage, and electrical systems had all failed; 32,000 sick and starving prisoners had been jammed into a space intended for one-third that number; and more than 39 railroad boxcars filled with dead people had been transported there for disposal.

The U.S. Army's 116th Evacuation Hospital was one of the first medical units to enter the camp after its liberation. As the 116th labored to restore civility and order to a world that had descended into barbarism and chaos, a young American medic, writing home to Michigan, struggled to describe a scene that lay beyond his worst imaginings.

Previous page: **Letter from Pfc. Harold Porter, a medic with the 116th Evacuation Hospital, to his parents, May 7, 1945, first page**

Using stationery found in the abandoned office of the camp commandant, Porter found himself at a loss to convey the horrors he encountered at the Dachau concentration camp: boxcars filled with thousands of decomposing bodies, the crematorium surrounded by stacks of nude corpses, and the stacks of carefully sorted clothing belonging to the victims.

His account is unsparing and graphic, with descriptions of what the bodies looked like, the sounds they made as they were being moved, and their odor. Days after entering the camp, he was still trying to grasp the reality of what he saw.

National Archives, Dwight D. Eisenhower Presidential Library and Museum, Abilene, Kansas. Courtesy of the Dwight D. Eisenhower Library, Sonya Porter Collection

Right: Railroad cars at Dachau concentration camp (detail), 1945

National Archives, Records of the Office of War Information (OWI) [208-AA-206-K16]

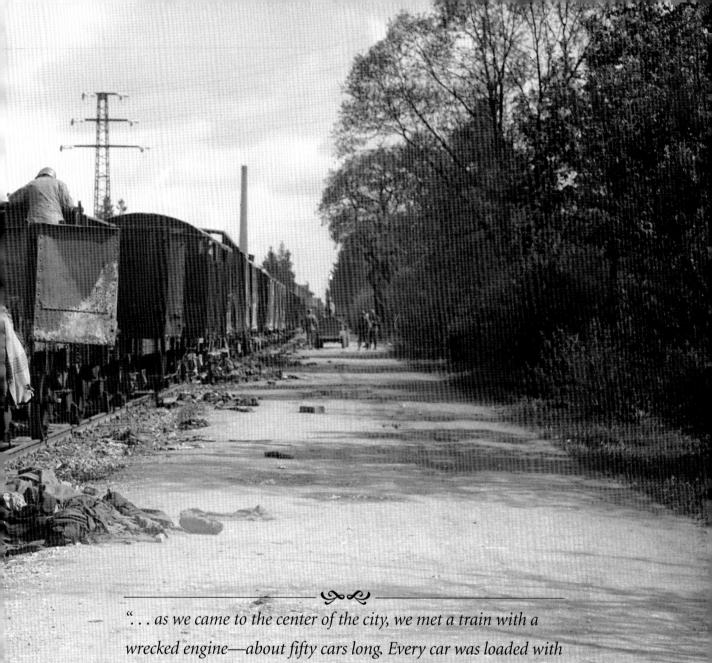

"... *as we came to the center of the city, we met a train with a wrecked engine—about fifty cars long. Every car was loaded with bodies. There must have been thousands of them—all obviously starved to death. This was a shock of the first order, and the odor can best be imagined. But neither the sight nor the odor were anything when compared with what we were still to see ...*"

—From Harold Porter's letter to his parents

207475

Gates at the main entrance to Dachau concentration camp, 1945
Reproduced courtesy of Keystone Picture Agency/ZUMA Press. National Archives, Records of the Office of War Information (OWI) [208-AA-206K-11]

"Tattered clothes from prisoners who were forced to strip before they were killed, lay in huge piles in the infamous Dachau concentration camp," 1945
National Archives, Records of the Office of the Chief Signal Officer [111-SC-206193]

"By this time I have recovered from my first emotional shock and am able to write without seeming like a hysterical gibbering idiot. Yet, I know you will hesitate to believe me no matter how objective and factual I try to be. I even find myself trying to deny what I am looking at with my own eyes . . . "

—From Harold Porter's letter to his parents

❧ Comdr. Jeremiah A. Denton, Jr.

Report from Inside a Hanoi Prison, 1966

"Whatever the position of my government is, 'I support it—fully. . ."

—Comdr. Jeremiah Denton, Jr., an American POW, responding to
an interviewer's question, May 2, 1966

On July 18, 1965, U.S. Navy Comdr. Jeremiah A. Denton, Jr., was shot down while leading an air attack on a military installation in North Vietnam. Captured by the North Vietnamese that day, he remained a prisoner of war for seven years and seven months, enduring years of solitary confinement and brutal mistreatment.

On May 2, 1966, as part of a propaganda campaign, the North Vietnamese arranged for him to be interviewed for television by a Japanese reporter. Asked about his views on the actions of the U.S. Government, he strongly affirmed his government's position, in defiance of his captors' instructions; he prepared himself for a torture session that was sure to follow.

While speaking on camera, he blinked in Morse code the word "T-O-R-T-U-R-E." Eventually, the videotape was widely circulated and reviewed by U.S. naval intelligence. Denton's one-word report, delivered in Morse code, was the first clear confirmation received by U.S. intelligence that American POWs were, in fact, being tortured.

He later speculated that the North Vietnamese did not learn of his blinking message until 1974. The taped interview is among the holdings of the Special Media Archives—Records of the Central Intelligence Agency.

Promoted during his captivity, Captain Denton was released on February 12, 1973. After retiring from the U.S. Navy as a rear admiral, he was elected to the U.S. Senate where he served from 1981 until 1987.

Comdr. Jeremiah Denton, Jr., photograph by Pomponio, March 1965
National Archives, General Records of the Department of the Navy, 1947–
[428-GX-831925]

Still frames from televised interview of Denton, May 2, 1966

Asked about his treatment, Denton responded—contrary to his thin and haggard appearance:

"I get adequate food and adequate clothing and medical care when I require it."

Asked about his views on the actions of the U.S. Government, he said:

"I don't know what is happening, but whatever the position of my government is, I support it—fully. Whatever the position of my government is, I believe in it—yes sir. I'm a member of that government and it is my job to support it, and I will as long as I live."

National Archives, Records of the Central Intelligence Agency

Free at Last

✺ John Boston

An Escape from Slavery, 1862

"My Dear Wife it is with grate joy I take this time to let you know Whare I am i am now in Safety in the 14th Regiment of Brooklyn …"

–John Boston, fugitive slave, 1862

The institution of slavery in America is older than the republic itself and so is the story of emancipation. Since colonial days, people held as slaves embraced American principles of liberty and equality as their own best hope for freedom and better treatment. Many acted as agents of their own liberation, claiming their freedom in the courts, in the military, and by fleeing to places where slavery did not exist.

By the onset of the Civil War in 1861, there were 3.9 million slaves in the United States. It was clear to them that slavery was at the heart of the national conflict, and with the nation at war, thousands saw an opportunity for freedom and seized it. Tearing themselves from their families, risking their lives, they fled to the Union Army offering themselves as workers, informants, and soldiers. In countless instances during the Civil War, emancipation was achieved one soul at a time, through extraordinary courage and at immeasurable cost.

In the midst of the Civil War, emancipation was pushed to the top of the nation's agenda as a moral imperative and military necessity. Congress formally proposed the thirteenth amendment outlawing slavery on January 31, 1865; it was ratified on December 6, 1865.

Pvt. Hubbard Pryor of Georgia, before and after his enlistment in the 44th U.S. Colored Infantry, 1864
National Archives, Records of the Adjutant General's Office, 1780's–1917

Letter from John Boston, a runaway slave, to his wife, Elizabeth, January 12, 1862

Fleeing slavery in Maryland, John Boston found refuge with a New York regiment in Upton Hill, Virginia, where he wrote this letter to his wife who remained in Owensville, Maryland. At the moment of celebrating his freedom, his highest hope and aspiration was to be reunited with his family.

There is no evidence that Elizabeth Boston ever received this letter. It was intercepted and eventually forwarded to Secretary of War Edwin Stanton. *National Archives, Records of the Adjutant General's Office, 1780's–1917*

"... this Day i can Adress you thank god as a free man   I had a little truble in giting away   But as the lord led the Children of Isrel to the land of Canon So he led me to a land Whare fredom Will rain in spite Of earth and hell   Dear you must make your Self content i am free from al the Slavers Lash ... I am With a very nice man and have All that hart Can Wish But My Dear I Cant express my grate desire that i Have to See you   i trust the time Will Come When We Shal meet again And if We dont met on earth We Will Meet in heven Whare Jesas ranes ..."

—From John Boston's letter to his wife

African American soldiers mustered out at Little Rock, Arkansas, detail from drawing by Alfred R. Waud, published in *Harper's Weekly*, May 19, 1866

Courtesy of the Library of Congress, Prints and Photographs Division, Washington, DC

❧ Chancellor Helmut Kohl
Reunification of Germany, 1990

"I am in Berlin. There were one million people here last night at the very spot where the Wall used to stand—and where President Reagan called on Mr. Gorbachev to open this gate. Words can't describe the feeling."

—German Chancellor Helmut Kohl, describing to President George H.W. Bush the celebration of German reunification in Berlin, October 3, 1990

Memo of telephone conversation between President George H.W. Bush and German Chancellor Helmut Kohl, October 3, 1990 President Bush phoned Chancellor Kohl to wish him well just hours after reunification went into effect. The conversation lasted approximately three minutes.
National Archives, George Bush Presidential Library and Museum, College Station, Texas

THE WHITE HOUSE
WASHINGTON   7876

MEMORANDUM OF TELEPHONE CONVERSATION

SUBJECT: Telephone Call to Chancellor Helmut Kohl of
                  Germany

PARTICIPANTS: The President
                  Helmut Kohl, Chancellor
                  Notetaker: Robert Hutchings, NSC Staff
                  Interpreter: Gisela Marcuse

DATE, TIME   October 3, 1990, 9:56 - 9:59 a.m.
AND PLACE: The Oval Office

The President: Helmut! I am sitting in a meeting with members of our Congress and am calling at the end of this historic day to wish you well.

Chancellor Kohl: Things are going very, very well. I am in Berlin. There were one million people here last night at the very spot where the Wall used to stand -- and where President Reagan called on Mr. Gorbachev to open this gate. Words can't describe the feeling. The weather is very nice and warm, fortunately. There were large crowds of young people. Eighty percent were under thirty. It was fantastic.

A short time ago there was enormous applause when our President said that our gratitude was owed especially to our Allied friends and above all our American friends. I share that view. When the parliamentary declaration is made, it will say that all American Presidents from Harry Truman all the way up to our friend George Bush made this possible. I would like to thank you again for all your support for us.

The President: It was covered widely on American television. America is proud to have stood with you through these negotiations, and we identify with the hopes of the German people. I have to run to another meeting, but I wanted you to know what pride we have in standing by the German people.

Chancellor Kohl: Thank you very much.

The President: Good-bye, my friend.

Chancellor Kohl: Tell your Congressmen good wishes and thanks.

-- End of Conversation --

After World War II, two German states came into existence following the occupation by the victorious Allied powers. The Federal Republic of Germany, known as West Germany, was established in the territory occupied by the non-Communist powers (United States, Britain, and France); the German Democratic Republic, known in the West as East Germany, was established in the zone occupied by the Soviet Union. Berlin, the former capital, was divided into West Berlin and East Berlin.

West Germany remained politically stable over the next forty years and became one of the most prosperous nations in the world. East Germany developed into a centralized Communist state whose citizens endured a stagnant economy and poor standard of living. By 1960, people were fleeing Soviet East Berlin for West Berlin and the non-Communist world at the rate of 30,000 each month. To stop this mass exodus, the Soviets built the Berlin Wall, which stood as a grim symbol of the gulf between the Communist East and the non-Communist West for twenty-eight years. In 1989, the Berlin Wall fell, signaling the end of the Cold War. The following year, the two German states, divided for forty-five years, were reunited in a joyful celebration ceremony that Chancellor Helmut Kohl described in the brief telephone conversation transcribed in this White House memo.

Reunification festivities at the Brandenburg Gate, photograph by Owen Franken, October 3, 1990
Some one million people in Berlin joyfully celebrated the moment of reunification at midnight with hymns, the peeling of a liberty bell, church bells, beer, and a special outdoor performance of Beethoven's Ninth Symphony ending with the choral celebration "Ode to Joy."
© Owen Franken/ CORBIS

President Bush on the telephone with German Chancellor Helmut Kohl during a meeting with congressmen at the White House, photograph by David Valdez, October 3, 1990
*National Archives, George Bush Presidential Library and Museum, College Station, Texas
[NLGB-P16308-10]*

❧ Theodore Joslin

President Herbert Hoover's Last Days in Office, 1933

"The people are more panic stricken today than at any time since the beginning of the depression."

—Theodore Joslin, secretary to President Herbert Hoover, February 28, 1933

President Herbert Hoover in the Oval Office with Theodore Joslin, 1932

National Archives, Herbert Hoover Presidential Library and Museum, West Branch, Iowa [NLHH-1932-10E]

Some of the most harrowing moments of the Great Depression came in the final weeks of President Herbert Hoover's administration with the collapse of the nation's banking system in February 1933. The imminent failure of two large banks in Michigan prompted that state's governor to declare a "banking holiday" on February 14, setting off a panic that soon infected the entire nation. During the last two weeks of Hoover's Presidency (Franklin D. Roosevelt was sworn into office on March 4), more than $1.2 billion was taken out of the nation's banks to be stored in mattresses, shoeboxes, and other hiding places believed to be more secure than the country's financial institutions.

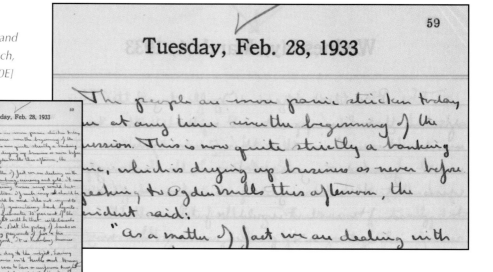

The fear and panic that gripped the nation reached all the way into the White House, where the President's secretary, Theodore Joslin, admitted to the President that he had withdrawn money from a Washington, DC, bank that he feared was on the brink of failure; the President urged Joslin to re-deposit the money in another bank.

Joslin's diary entry recounts that conversation.

❧❧

"The Commercial [Bank] did open this morning and although I felt unpatriotic in doing so, I drew out most of the money in my checking account and had Rowena come in and withdraw her savings account. And I told the President what I had done.

'Don't hoard it, Ted,' was his only comment. 'Put it in another bank that is safe. I would suggest the Riggs. It is the most liquid.' But I am 'hoarding' temporarily. No bank is really liquid today and won't be until this panic is over. The daily hoarding figures from the Treasury are gastly. That of yesterday was $165,000,000, bringing the total to in excess of $2,200,000,000 . . ."

——From Theodore Joslin's diary

❧❧

৵ George H.W. Bush

President Richard Nixon's Last Hours in Office, 1974

"The speech was vintage Nixon–a kick or two at the press… One couldn't help but look at the family and the whole thing and think of his accomplishments and then think of the shame and wonder what kind of a man is this really."

—George H.W. Bush, Chairman of the Republican National
Committee, August 9, 1974

Opposite page:
President Richard Nixon, flanked by his family, delivering his farewell remarks to the White House staff in the East Room of the White House, photograph by Karl Schumacher, August 9, 1974
National Archives, Nixon Presidential Materials Staff, College Park, Maryland [NLNS-E3392C-13]

During the night of June 17, 1972, five burglars broke into the office of the Democratic National Committee at the Watergate office complex in Washington, DC. Investigation into the break-in exposed a trail of abuses that led to the highest levels of the Nixon administration and ultimately to the President himself. President Nixon resigned from office under threat of impeachment on August 9, 1974.

A historic day of transition, August 9 was marked by two milestone events at the White House: President Nixon became the first President in U.S. history to resign the office, and Vice President Ford, who had never campaigned for the office of Vice President or President was sworn in as President (while serving as Speaker of the House, Ford was chosen by Nixon to be Vice President when Spiro T. Agnew resigned the office in 1973). At 9:36 a.m., Nixon made his farewell remarks to the Cabinet and White House staff. At 12:05 p.m., Gerald Ford was sworn in as 38th President of the United States. George Herbert Walker Bush, then Chairman of the Republican National Committee, was present at both events. He composed this diary account, noting how the tears and grief of Nixon's farewell, gave way to a cheerier, forward-looking "new spirit" at Ford's swearing-in.

Cox in the Rose Garden – talked to them on the way into the ceremony.
President Nixon looked just awful. He used glasses – the first time I
ever saw them. Close to breaking down – understandably. Everyone in the
room in tears. The speech was vintage Nixon – a kick or two at the
press – enormous strains. One couldn't help but look at the family and
the whole thing and think of his accomplishments and then think of the
shame and wonder what kind of a man is this really. No morality – kicking
his friends in those tapes – all of them. Gratuitous abuse. Caring for
no one and yet doing so much. When he used the word 'plumbers' meaning
it 'laboring with his hands' the connotation was a shock on me. I remember
Lt. Col. Brennan who has been with him so long – Marine – standing proudly
but with tears running down his face. Rabbi Korff, a brand new friend
on the scene who told Kendall he wanted to start a Support for Ford
Committee. Thrilled with the limelight. Coming in and standing around
and looking for special attention, ending up sitting next to the Cabinet.
People who labored next to Nixon's side forever are not invited. It's
weird. The Nixon speech was masterful. In spite of his inability to
totally resist a dig at the press, that argument about hating – only if
you hate do you join the haters. We walked through the bottom lobby to
go out. After the Ford swearing-in many of the pictures were changed with
a great emphasis on the new President. We went over and hung around waiting
for the swearing in of Ford.

President, and his wife, Pat Burch;
[Patrick J.] Buchanan, assistant to President Nixon;
Tricia and "Eddie" Cox, President Nixon's
daughter and son-in-law; and
Rabbi [Baruch] Korff, Chairman, Citizens
Committee for Fairness to the Presidency.
*National Archives, George Bush Presidential
Library and Museum, College Station, Texas*

"President Nixon looked just awful. He used glasses—the first time I ever saw them. Close to breaking down—understandably. Everyone in the room in tears . . . I remember Lt. Col. Brennan who has been with him so long—Marine— standing proudly but with tears running down his face. . . . The Nixon speech was masterful. In spite of his inability to totally resist a dig at the press, that argument about hating— only if you hate do you join the haters. We walked through the bottom lobby to go out. . . . We went over and hung around waiting for the swearing in of Ford.

And then the whole mood changed. It was quiet, respectful, sorrowful in one sense, but upbeat. The music and the band seemed cheerier, the talking and babbling of voices after Ford's fantastic speech, crowds of friends, indeed a new spirit, a new lift . . ."

—From George H.W. Bush's diary

Below: President Ford delivering remarks in the East Room of the White House moments after being sworn in, photograph by David Hume Kennerly, August 9, 1974
National Archives, Gerald R. Ford Library, Ann Arbor, Michigan [NLGRF-AV95-4-238-1]

Opposite page: Richard Nixon departs from the White House before Gerald Ford was sworn in as President, photograph by Oliver F. Atkins, August 9, 1974
National Archives, Nixon Presidential Materials Staff, College Park, Maryland [NLNS-E3398-09]

♂ **Robert King Stone**

Assassination of President Abraham Lincoln, 1865

"I was sent for by Mrs. Lincoln immediately after the assassination. I arrived there in a very few moments . . ."

—Dr. Robert King Stone, President Lincoln's family physician, who treated the President after he was shot on April 14, 1865

Dr. Robert King Stone, photograph from the Mathew Brady Collection, ca. 1861–65
National Archives, Records of the Office of the Chief Signal Officer [111-B-5927]

On April 14, 1865, at approximately 10:20 p.m., John Wilkes Booth, a prominent American actor, snuck up behind President Abraham Lincoln as he watched a play at Ford's Theater, and shot him in the back of the head at point-blank range. The President was carried across the street to a private home where he died early the following morning. Booth, pursued by Union soldiers for twelve days through southern Maryland and Virginia, died of a gunshot wound on April 26 after refusing to surrender to Federal troops.

The murder of President Lincoln was part of a larger conspiracy that included a simultaneous attack on Secretary of State William H. Seward and the possible targeting of Vice President Andrew Johnson. Assuming the Presidency after Lincoln's death, President Johnson considered the crime a military one, and he ordered that the eight accused conspirators be tried before a military commission. Dr. Robert King Stone, the Lincoln family physician, was one of 350 witnesses who testified during the course of the proceedings. His testimony is shown here.

Dr. Robert King Stone,

a witness called for the prosecution, being duly sworn, testified as follows:

By the Judge Advocate

Q. State to the Court if you are a practising physician in this city?
A. I am.
Q. Were you, or not, the physician of the late President of the United States?
A. I was his family physician.
Q. State whether or not you were called to see him on the evening of his assassination, and the examination which you made, and the Result?
A. I was sent for by Mrs Lincoln immediately after the assassination. I arrived there in a very few moments and found that the President had

Below: Abraham Lincoln, photograph from the Mathew Brady Collection, ca. 1861–65
National Archives, Records of the Office of the Chief Signal Officer [111-B-3658]

Statement of Dr. Robert King Stone, President Lincoln's family physician, May 16, 1865, first page
The eight accused conspirators were tried before a military tribunal that convened at the old penitentiary on the grounds of the Washington Arsenal, the site presently occupied by Fort McNair. Court reporters took down verbatim the testimony of each witness in shorthand. This document is a transcription of Dr. Stone's testimony, as recorded by the court reporters.

Of the fourteen doctors who attended President Lincoln on the night of his assassination, Dr. Stone is the only one who presented testimony on the President's condition. *National Archives, Records of the Office of the Judge Advocate General (Army)*

President Lincoln's deathbed, photograph by Julius Ulke, April 15, 1865

Six men carried the President across the street to the back bedroom of a house owned by William Petersen. There the doctors monitored his breathing and vital signs throughout the night. All of the doctors in attendance were convinced that the wound was fatal. Only Mrs. Lincoln, stunned and inconsolable, clung to hope for his recovery. The President died the following morning at 7:22 a.m.

Julius Ulke, who was a boarder at the house where Lincoln died, took this photograph shortly after the President's body was removed. *Courtesy of Chicago History Museum [ICHi-11209], Chicago, Illinois*

"... [I] found that the President had been removed from the theatre to the house of a gentleman living directly opposite the theatre, had been carried into the back room of the residence, and was there placed upon a bed. I found a number of gentlemen, citizens, around him ... I proceeded then to examine him, and instantly found that the President had received a gun shot wound in the back part of the left side of his head, into which I carried immediately my finger. I at once informed those around that the case was a hopeless one; that the President would die; that there was no positive limit to the duration of his life, that his vital tenacity was very strong, and he would resist as long as any man could, but that death certainly would soon close the scene. I remained with him doing whatever was in my power, assisted by my friends, to aid him, but of course, nothing could be done, and he died the next morning at about half past seven o'clock ..."

—From Dr. Stone's testimony

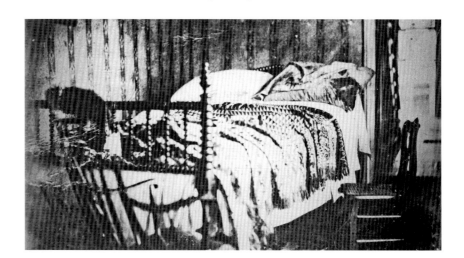

✿ Lady Bird Johnson

Assassination of President John F. Kennedy, 1963

"I cast one last look over my shoulder and saw in the President's car, a bundle of pink, just like a drift of blossoms, lying on the back seat. I think it was Mrs. Kennedy lying over the President's body."

—Lady Bird Johnson, diary entry for November 22, 1963

On November 22, 1963, at approximately 12:30 p.m., local time, President John F. Kennedy was shot in Dallas, Texas, while riding in a motorcade with his wife, Jacqueline Kennedy, Texas Governor John Connally, and his wife, Nelly Connally. The motorcade rushed to Parkland Hospital where, at 1 p.m., the President was pronounced dead.

Vice President Lyndon Johnson and his wife, Lady Bird Johnson, were also riding in the motorcade, two cars behind the President's car. Unharmed, they too were rushed to the hospital. On the death of President Kennedy, Lyndon Johnson became President of the United States. He was sworn in at approximately 2:30 p.m., on board Air Force One, moments before returning to Washington, DC, with Mrs. Kennedy and the late President's casket on board.

At her husband's side, Lady Bird Johnson found herself at the center of the tragic events that brought the country to a standstill. Two or three days after the assassination, she recorded her recollections. Speaking slowly, choosing her words carefully—and with the sensibilities of a poet—she told what she saw and gave voice to the heartbreak of a day that is emblazoned in our national memory.

President and Mrs. Kennedy deplane from Air Force One at Love Field in Dallas, photograph by Cecil Stoughton, November 22, 1963
National Archives, John F. Kennedy Presidential Library and Museum, Boston, Massachusetts [NLJFK-WHP-ST-STC420-51-63]

President and Mrs. Kennedy arrive at Dallas (detail), photograph by Cecil Stoughton, November 22, 1963
National Archives, John F. Kennedy Presidential Library and Museum, Boston, Massachusetts [NLJFK-WHP-ST-STC420-13-63]

Transcript of Lady Bird Johnson's audio diary from November 22, 1963, first page
So detailed were Mrs. Johnson's observations, this typed transcript of her tape-recorded account served as her official statement to the Warren Commission, the body created to investigate the assassination of President Kennedy.

Some of the hand-written notes are in the hand of Mrs. Johnson; others are in the hand of Abe Fortas, a prominent Washington, DC, attorney and close friend of the Johnsons who often advised them. *National Archives, Lyndon Baines Johnson Library and Museum, Austin, Texas*

Mary for many years had been in charge of altering the clothes which I purchased at a Dallas trip—

Transcript from Mrs. Johnson's tapes of November 22, 1963

(relating to)

It all began so beautifully. After a drizzle in the morning, the sun came out bright and beautiful. We were going into Dallas. In the lead car, President and Mrs. Kennedy, John and Nellie, and then a Secret Service car full of men, and then our car - Lyndon and me and Senator Yarborough. The streets were lined with people - lots and lots of people - the children all smiling, placards, confetti, people waving from windows. One last happy moment I had was looking up and seeing Mary Griffith leaning out of a window waving at me. Then almost at the edge of town, on our way to the Trade Mart where we were going to have the luncheon, we were rounding a curve, going down a hill and suddenly there was a sharp loud report - a shot. It seemed to me to come from the right above my shoulder from a building. Then a moment and then two more shots in rapid succession. There had been such a gala air that I thought it must be firecrackers or some sort of celebration. Then in the lead car, the Secret Service men were suddenly down. I heard over the radio system, "Let's get out of here," and our man who was with us, Ruf Youngblood, I believe it was, vaulted over the front seat on top of Lyndon, threw him to the floor, and said, "Get down." Senator Yarborough and I ducked our heads. The car accelerated terrifically fast - faster and faster. Then suddenly they put on the brakes so hard that I wondered if they were going to make it as the wheel left as we went around the corner. We pulled up to a building. I looked up and saw it said "Hospital." Only then did I believe that this might be what it was. Yarborough kept on saying in an excited voice, "Have they shot the President?" I said something l As we ground to a halt - we were still the t Service men began to pull, lead, guide and h one last look over my shoulder and saw a bun a drift of blossoms lying on the back seat.

Lady Bird Johnson working on her diary in the second floor bedroom of the White House, photograph by Robert Knudsen, November 15, 1968
Mrs. Johnson's account of November 22, 1963, proved to be the first entry of an audio diary that Mrs. Johnson maintained throughout her years as First Lady. *National Archives, Lyndon Baines Johnson Library and Museum, Austin, Texas [NLLBJ-D2440-7a]*

". . . Suddenly I found myself face to face with Jackie in a small hall. I think it was right outside the operating room. You always think of her—or someone like her as being insulated, protected—she was quite alone. I don't think I ever saw anyone so much alone in my life."

——From Lady Bird Johnson's diary

ॐ **President Harry S. Truman**

President Truman Meets Soviet
Marshal Joseph Stalin, 1945

"I looked up from the desk and there stood Stalin in the doorway . . ."

—President Harry S. Truman at the Potsdam Conference, July 17, 1945

Soviet Marshal Joseph Stalin and President Truman (detail), July 17, 1945

National Archives, Records of the Office of the Chief Signal Officer [111-SC-209221-S]

On July 17, 1945, two months after Germany surrendered to the Allies at the end of World War II, President Harry S. Truman came face to face with Marshal Joseph Stalin of the Soviet Union, one of the most brutal autocrats of all time.

The meeting between Truman and Stalin took place in a suburb of the devastated city of Berlin just before the opening of the Potsdam Conference. Truman, Stalin, and Great Britain's Prime Minister Winston Churchill, leaders of the three largest Allied nations, were gathered there to discuss the political future of Europe and the conduct of the war still raging in the Pacific. Having assumed the Presidency just three months earlier, Truman had not met "Mr. Russia" and "Mr. Great Britain," as he privately referred to his Allied partners, and was looking forward to the conference as an opportunity to establish a personal rapport with them.

Stalin came to call on the President at noon. Truman was unruffled and spoke plainly. After the meeting, which lasted two hours, Stalin stayed for lunch. Later that afternoon, Truman scribbled this account for his diary, satisfied that the Soviet leader was someone he could deal with.

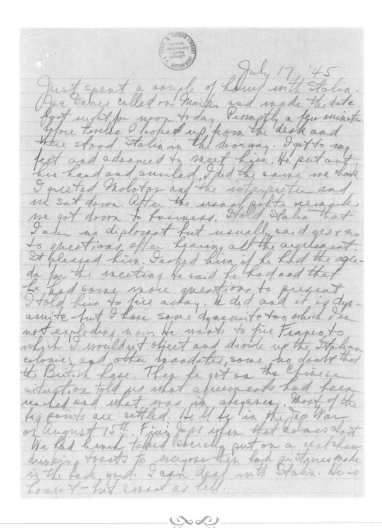

President Harry S. Truman's diary, July 17, 1945
The night before this meeting, President Truman learned that the United States had successfully tested the world's first atomic bomb in the desert sands of New Mexico near Alamogordo, which probably explains the diary's cryptic reference to "dynamite." *National Archives, Harry S. Truman Presidential Library and Museum, Independence, Missouri*

Opposite page bottom: **Hand-carved desk used by President Truman at the "Little White House" where he stayed during the Potsdam Conference, photograph by Lieutenant Newell, July 13, 1945**
National Archives, Records of the Office of the Chief Signal Officer [111-SC-209521-S]

"Promptly a few minutes before twelve I looked up from the desk and there stood Stalin in the doorway. I got to my feet and advanced to meet him. He put out his hand and smiled. I did the same … After the usual polite remarks we got down to business. I told Stalin that I am no diplomat but usually said yes or no to questions after hearing all the argument. It pleased him. I asked him if he had the agenda for the meeting. He said he had and that he had some more questions to present. I told him to fire away. He did and it is dynamite—but I have some dynamite too which I'm not exploding now … I can deal with Stalin. He is honest—but smart as hell."

—*From President Truman's diary*

❧ Alonzo Fields

Dinner for the President and His Advisors, 1950

"At about 4:P.M. Sunday, June 25 . . . the usher on duty called me excitedly saying the President was returning and wanted cocktails and dinner at 8:00 P.M. . . ."

—Alonzo Fields, Chief Butler at the White House, 1950

On Saturday, June 24, 1950, while enjoying a family weekend in Independence, Missouri, President Harry S. Truman learned that North Korea had invaded South Korea. The next day, he flew back to Washington, DC, and called an emergency meeting of senior officials to be held at Blair House that evening. (Blair House was the President's official residence while the White House was undergoing renovation.)

The President's emergency meeting precipitated a crisis for another leader in the nation's capital, Alonzo Fields, Chief Butler at the White House, who also had been enjoying the afternoon off; with the President and First Family out of town, Fields had dismissed the White House kitchen staff until Monday morning. At 4 p.m., Fields received a call from the White House usher, informing him that fourteen of the President's senior advisors would soon assemble at Blair House for dinner. The guests would arrive for cocktails and hors d'oeuvres at 8 p.m.; dinner would be served at 8:30 p.m., when the President was expected to arrive.

Fields sprang into action. Marshaling his forces with the help of Washington, DC, police who located two of the White House cooks, he headed to Blair House, composing along the way a menu based on his recollection of the food supplies on hand. The butler who was to help Fields serve the meal arrived only five minutes before the guests.

Alonzo Fields, not dated

Alonzo Fields was butler, chief butler, and maitre d' at the White House from 1931 to 1953. With a young family to support, Alonzo Fields, who had trained as a classical singer at the New England Conservatory of Music, gave up his chance of a musical career and took a job as a butler at the White House in 1931. During his tenure there, he considered himself privileged to observe the most influential people of the time at close range.

But his dream of a singing career persisted. He looked back at his twenty-one years of White House service and remembered as his greatest thrill, the day he performed in the East Room of the White House, at the Christmas Party held in 1932 for the mansion's domestic staff. *Courtesy of the Smithsonian Center for Folklife and Cultural Heritage, Washington, DC*

Sunday, June 25, 1950 was like so many days in June in Washington, hot and muggy. President Truman was away in Independence for a long week end. Mrs. Truman alwsys left early in June for Independence.With the President being away. I closed the kitchen for the week end, with orders for all kitchen helpand butlers to check in with me at noon Sunday,then I should know if the President would returning. So at noon Sunday, I cleared everyone until breakfast call Monday,June 26 1950.

At about 4:P.M. Sunday,June 25,Mr Claunch, the usher on duty called me excitedly saying that the President was returning and wanted cocktails and dinner at 8:00 P.M.for the Sec. of State and the Army,Navy and Airforce chiefs of Staffs,and for me not to wait on him, but to start serving the guest codktails upon their arrivals.He was not sure how many to expect, perhaps 18 or 20. I suggested to Mr.Claunch,if possible to have radio and police calls made to summon the help to report to the White House. I planned dinner in the cab on my way to theWhite House, in respect to the su pplies I had on hand.. I cooked,set the table,made canapes for cocktails , until the first cook arrive at 6:00 P.M. which gave me leave to continue setting the table,My first butler arrived at &x 7:45 and the guest started to arrive 7:50.Secretary Acheson and General Omar Bradleywas were the first to arrive. The President arrived at 8:30 and we preceded with the dinner that started the conference in making the decision to take police action in Korea.

Notes of Alonzo Fields, Chief White House Butler, on the June 25, 1950, dinner for the President and his advisors

While the President, the Secretary of State, the Secretary of Defense, the Joint Chiefs of Staff, and eight other officials discussed the crisis in Korea that evening, they dined on fruit cup, fried chicken, shoestring potatoes, buttered asparagus, scalloped tomatoes, hot biscuits, hearts of lettuce, vanilla ice cream with chocolate sauce, and cupcakes. Within days, the American people learned that the United States had committed its military forces to help defend South Korea. Alonzo Fields wrote these notes on the preparations for that historic dinner. *National Archives, Harry S. Truman Presidential Library and Museum, Independence, Missouri*

War at Sea

❧ Lt. Thomas O. Selfridge, Jr.

Sinking of the USS *Cumberland*, 1862

"The dead were thrown over the other side of the deck, the wounded carried below: no one flinched but went on loading and firing, taking the place of some comrade killed or wounded as they had been taught to do. But the carnage was something awful . . ."

—Lt. Thomas O. Selfridge, Jr., crew member of the USS *Cumberland*,
   sunk by the Confederate ironclad CSS *Virginia* on March 8, 1862

On Saturday, March 8, 1862, one year after the onset of the Civil War, the crewmen of the Union blockade squadron standing off at Hampton Roads, Virginia, had grown bored waiting for the enemy's arrival. While the laundry hung on the Union ships' rigging drying in the midday sun, the Confederate ironclad CSS *Virginia* steamed slowly from Norfolk toward the Union fleet. Until that day, no one knew how an ironclad would perform in battle against a fleet of wooden ships.

The engagement began close to 3 p.m. When it was over, before dark, the USS *Cumberland* was sunk, the USS *Minnesota* had been forced aground, and the USS *Congress* surrendered and then was burned. With the support of the Confederate gunships CSS *Beaufort* and CSS *Raleigh*, the *Virginia* had devastated the Union fleet, signaling that the era of wooden battleships would soon come to an end.

The USS *Cumberland* was fired upon, rammed, and sunk, in a dramatic demonstration of the ironclad's superiority in battle. The gallantry of the *Cumberland's* crew—who fought beyond all hope, refusing to surrender even as their ship went down—was immortalized in poems by Herman Melville, Henry Wadsworth Longfellow, and others. Lt. Thomas O. Selfridge, Jr., who commanded one of the ship's gun divisions, survived the battle, and wrote this vivid and graphic account of it twenty-three years later.

Rear Adm. Thomas O. Selfridge, Jr., not dated
National Archives, Records of the Bureau of Ships [19-N-13128]

The Sinking of the Cumberland, hand-colored lithograph by F. Newman, published by Currier & Ives, ca. 1862

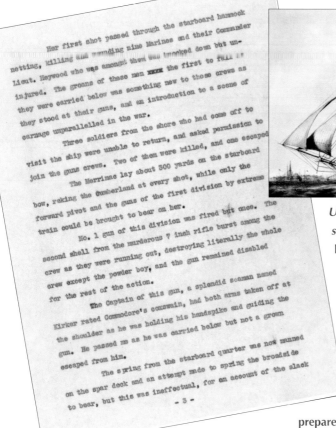

Her first shot passed through the starboard hammock netting, killing and wounding nine Marines and their Commander Lieut. Heywood who was amongst them was knocked down but uninjured. The groans of these men were the first to fall in they were carried below was something new to those crews as they stood at their guns, and an introduction to a scene of carnage unparallelled in the war.

Three soldiers from the shore who had come off to visit the ship were unable to return, and asked permission to join the guns crews. Two of them were killed, and one escaped

The Merrimac lay about 300 yards on the starboard bow, raking the Cumberland at every shot, while only the forward pivot and the guns of the first division by extreme train could be brought to bear on her.

No. 1 gun of this division was fired but once. The second shell from the murderous 7 inch rifle burst among the crew as they were running out, destroying literally the whole crew except the powder boy, and the gun remained disabled for the rest of the action.

The Captain of this gun, a splendid seaman named Kirker rated Commodore's coxswain, had both arms taken off at the shoulder as he was holding his handspike and guiding the gun. He passed me as he was carried below but not a groan escaped from him.

The spring from the starboard quarter was now manned on the spar deck and an attempt made to spring the broadside to bear, but this was ineffectual, for an account of the slack

- 3 -

U.S. Frigate Cumberland, 54 Guns. The flag ship of the Gulf Squadron, Com. Perry, lithograph by N. Currier, 1843

Selfridge described the *Cumberland* as "a splendid type of the frigate of the old times, with her towering masts, long yards, and neat man-of-war like appearance." *Courtesy of the U.S. Navy Art Collection, Washington, DC*

"From an Address on the 'Cumberland' prepared by Admiral Selfridge," 1885, selected page

Selfridge pays tribute to the seamen on board the *Cumberland* who continued to work their guns even as their comrades fell and their ship began to sink. He conveys the grisly chaos of nineteenth-century naval warfare: the noise of the guns, the smoke of the gunfire, the decks awash with blood and littered with the body parts of the fallen.

Of the 376 men known to be aboard the *Cumberland* on March 8, 121 were killed. *National Archives, Naval Records Collection of the Office of Naval Records and Library*

CSS *Virginia*, wash drawing by Clary Ray, 1898

In 1861, the Confederates salvaged the USS *Merrimack*, which Federal forces had scuttled and burned when forced to abandon the Navy Yard in Norfolk, and converted her into an ironclad that they christened the CSS *Virginia*. Many people, including Selfridge, continued to refer to the ironclad as the *Merrimack*.

Although the CSS *Virginia* prevailed on March 8, 1862, she did not escape unscathed: her iron ram was lost, her stack riddled, and two large guns were put out of order. *Courtesy of the U.S. Navy Art Collection, Washington, DC*

✎✎

"Her first shot passed through the starboard hammock netting, killing and wounding nine Marines and their Commander . . . The groans of these men the first to fall as they were carried below was something new to those crews as they stood at their guns, and an introduction to a scene of carnage unparallelled in the war . . .

The Captain of [the No. 1 gun], a splendid seaman named Kirker rated Commodore's coxswain, had both arms taken off at the shoulder as he was holding his handspike and guiding the gun. He passed me as he was carried below but not a grown escaped from him. . . .

. . . Every 1st and 2nd captains of the guns of the first division was killed or wounded, and the writer with a box of cannon primers in his pocket went from gun to gun firing them as fast as the decimated crews could load them. . . .

Seeing that our shot made so little impression, the gun captains were ordered to fire only at the ports.

The Merrimac hailed the Cumberland and asked if she would surrender, the reply went back 'Never, we will sink with our colors flying . . .' "

—From Admiral Selfridge's account

✎✎

❧ Kapitänleutnant Walter Schwieger
Sinking of the RMS *Lusitania*, 1915

"In the distance straight ahead a number of life-boats were moving; nothing more was to be seen of the 'Lusitania.'"

—Kapitänleutnant Walter Schwieger, Commander of the German submarine that sank the *Lusitania*, May 7, 1915

Kapitänleutnant Walter Schwieger, not dated

Schwieger was an aggressive and skillful naval officer. In 1917, he received the highest honor that a German naval officer could receive. He died at sea that September when his U-boat struck a mine. *Courtesy of Bundesarchiv, Freiburg, Germany*

"Travellers intending to embark on the Atlantic voyage are reminded that a state of war exists between Germany . . . and Great Britain . . . and that travellers sailing in the war zone on ships of Great Britain or her allies do so at their own risk."

So read a notice from the German government that ran in forty U.S. newspapers on May 1, 1915, ten months after the outbreak of World War I and three months after Germany declared a submarine blockade of the British Isles. On that day, the British luxury liner, the RMS *Lusitania*, set sail from New York for Liverpool; six days later, twelve miles off the southern coast of Ireland, she was torpedoed by a German submarine and sank. Of the 1,959 people on board, 1,195 died, including more than 120 Americans.

In the context of a wartime crossing, the cargo of the *Lusitania* on her last voyage included war materiel for the Allied war effort, including 52 tons of shrapnel shells, more than 3,000 percussion fuses, and 4,200 cases of Remington rifle cartridges.

Kapitänleutnant Walter Schwieger was the thirty-year-old commander of the submarine *U-20* that sank the *Lusitania*. His war diary describes the attack and the rapid sinking of the great liner as he viewed it through his periscope.

Below, right: **War diary of Kapitänleutnant Walter Schwieger recording the attack and sinking of the *Lusitania*, May 7, 1915, title page**

This copy of Schwieger's diary came to the Department of the Navy (and, eventually, to the National Archives) through the U.S. Army's Military Intelligence Division.

In the diary, typed from his handwritten notes, Schwieger stated that he caught sight of the *Lusitania* in the distance, while his submarine was surfaced; he quickly submerged his vessel, moved into an attack position, and at 3:10 p.m., ordered the launch of the torpedo from a distance of 700 meters.

The diary chronicles the chaos and panic he observed while the ship's crew and passengers tried to put the lifeboats in the water as the ship listed sharply starboard. The ship sank after eighteen minutes; only six of the forty-eight lifeboats had made it safely into the water.

The cause of the explosion on board the *Lusitania* has been the subject of study and debate since 1915. Experts tend to agree now that the explosion was caused by an industrial accident (likely the detonation of coal dust or aluminum powder ignited by fire resulting from the torpedo hit), rather than the combustion of explosive munitions on board. *National Archives, Naval Records Collection of the Office of Naval Records and Library*

Below: **Lusitania, not dated**

According to experts, the *Lusitania* could have stayed afloat after it was hit, long enough for passengers to safely get in the lifeboats, had the explosion not occurred.

The sinking of the *Lusitania* triggered an international backlash of public opinion against Germany for killing a large number of innocent civilians.
Courtesy of the Library of Congress, Prints and Photographs Division, Washington, DC

Torpedoed *Lusitania*, drawing printed in *New York Herald* and *London Sphere*, ca. 1915
Courtesy of the Library of Congress, Prints and Photographs Division, Washington, DC

"Clear bow shot at 700 [meters] . . . Shot struck starboard side close behind the bridge. An extraordinarily heavy detonation followed, with a very large cloud of smoke (far above the front funnel). A second explosion must have followed that of the torpedo (boiler or coal or powder?). . . . The ship stopped immediately and quickly listed sharply to starboard, sinking deeper by the head at the same time. It appeared as if it would capsize in a short time. Great confusion arose on the ship; some of the boats were swung clear and lowered into the water. Many people must have lost their heads; several boats loaded with people rushed downward, struck the water bow or stern first and filled at once. . . . The ship blew off steam; at the bow the name "Lusitania" in golden letters was visible. The funnels were painted black; stern flag not in place. It was running 20 nautical miles. Since it seemed as if the steamer could only remain above water for a short time, went to 24 m. and ran toward the Sea. Nor could I have fired a second torpedo into this swarm of people who were trying to save themselves."

—From an official translation of Schwieger's diary

Personal Encounters

✑ John Adams

Audience with King George III, 1785

"I went with his Lordship thro' the Levee Room—into the King's Closet. The door was shut and I was left with his Majesty and the Secretary of State alone."

—John Adams, describing his audience with King George, June 2, 1785

John Adams, painting by John Singleton Copley, 1783

Courtesy of the Harvard University Portrait Collection, Boston, Massachusetts, Bequest of Ward Nicholas Boylston to Harvard College, 1828 H74

On July 4, 1776, John Adams, delegate to the Continental Congress from Massachusetts, voted to adopt the Declaration of Independence, proclaiming the British King unfit to be ruler of a free people. The King had proclaimed the rebellious colonists to be traitors. Could Adams possibly have imagined that, after eight years of warfare, he would stand before that same King, as a respected diplomat on the world stage, presenting his credentials as the first United States Minister Plenipotentiary to Britain?

On June 1, 1785, King George formally received John Adams, representative of the fledgling nation that had dealt the British Empire a bitter defeat. The meeting, as Adams recounted in this official account, was marked by the pomp and ceremony required by the occasion of a royal audience. But beneath the pageantry, Adams described a strong undercurrent of emotion as the King and his former subject—who once reviled each other as bitter enemies—met face to face, as statesmen.

Opposite: *George III*, **oil painting by studio of Allan Ramsay, London, England, ca. 1770**

Courtesy of Colonial Williamsburg Foundation, Williamsburg, Virginia

Page 56, bottom right: **Letter from John Adams, Minister to Britain, to John Jay, Secretary of State, reporting on his audience with the King, June 2, 1785, selected page**

John Adams arrived in London on May 26, 1785, to assume the post of the first United States Minister Plenipotentiary to Britain. Less than one week later, he went to St. James Palace to present his credentials to the King.

This letter is Adams's official report on that extraordinary meeting. It includes the remarks that Adams made (a speech he had rehearsed and committed to memory) and, as best as he could remember, the words spoken by the King in reply. *National Archives, Records of the Continental and Confederation Congresses and the Constitutional Convention*

John Adams's remarks to King George III

"Sir, The United States of America have appointed me their Minister Plenipotentiary to your Majesty . . . It is in Obedience to their express Commands that I have the Honor to assure your Majesty of their unanimous Disposition and Desire to cultivate the most friendly and liberal Intercourse between your Majesty's Subjects and their Citizens . . . The appointment of a Minister from the United States to your Majesty's Court, will form an Epocha in the History of England & of America. I think myself more fortunate than all my fellow Citizens in having the distinguished Honor to be the first to stand in your Majesty's royal Presence in a diplomatic Character . . ."

Response of King George III

"I wish you Sir, to believe, and that it may be understood in America, that I have done nothing in the late Contest, but what I thought myself indispensably bound to do, by the Duty which I owed to my People. I will be very frank with you. I was the last to consent to the Separation, but the Separation having been made and having become inevitable, I have always said, as I say now, that I would be the first to meet the Friendship of the United States as an independent Power. . . let the Circumstances of Language; Religion and Blood have their natural and full Effect."

❧ Rose Kennedy

Ambassador and Mrs. Joseph Kennedy
at Windsor Castle, 1938

"After a few minutes of contemplating the scene, Joe turned to me and said, 'Rose, this is a hell of a long way from East Boston.'"

—Rose Kennedy's diary chronicling a visit to Windsor Castle, April 1938

In December 1937, Joseph Kennedy, father of the future President, John F. Kennedy, was appointed U.S. Ambassador to Great Britain. It was among the most prestigious of all the diplomatic posts—one he had lobbied for over many months. When he and his large, rambunctious family arrived in London in March 1938, English society welcomed them with open arms.

In London, the American Ambassador and his wife soared to the heights of British society. In the spring of 1938, just before war would cast its shadow across Europe, the couple luxuriated in the warmth of English hospitality, hobnobbing with aristocrats and royalty at the many balls, dinners, regattas, and derbies of the season. The highlight was surely the April weekend that they spent at Windsor Castle, guests of King George VI and his wife, Queen Elizabeth. In great detail, Rose Kennedy chronicled those unforgettable days in her diary.

Rose Kennedy's account of the weekend at Windsor Castle, April 9–11, 1938, first page

Mrs. Kennedy's account reads like a fairy tale, complete with footmen, ladies-in-waiting, lavish gowns, sumptuous meals, and glittering jewels.

Other guests at Windsor Castle that weekend included Prime Minister Neville Chamberlain, Mrs. Chamberlain, Lord Halifax (Foreign Secretary), Lady Halifax, Lord Elphinstone, and Lady Elphinstone, sister of the Queen. *National Archives, John F. Kennedy Presidential Library and Museum, Boston, Massachusetts, Rose Kennedy Papers Collection, Courtesy of the John F. Kennedy Library Foundation.*

WINDSOR CASTLE

WE CAME UP FROM LONDON IN AN EMBASSY CAR FROM WINDSOR AND DROVE THROUGH A LARGE AND BEAUTIFUL PARK TO ARRIVE AT THE CASTLE AT 7:00 P.M. THERE WE WERE MET BY THE MASTER OF THE HOUSEHOLD, BRIG. GENERAL SIR HILL CHILD, WHO CONDUCTED US TO OUR ROOMS. THEY WERE IN ONE OF THE TOWERS WITH A LOVELY VIEW OF THE PARK, AND WERE UPHOLSTERED IN RED DAMASK & WHITE LINEN PAPER. THERE WERE ACCESSORIES IN GOLD AND WHITE. IN MY BEDROOM WAS A HUGE BED, ALSO UPHOLSTERED IN RED DAMASK AND SET HIGH, SO ONE HAD TO USE A STEP STOOL TO ENTER IT. THERE WERE NUMEROUS SERVANTS IN EVIDENCE, IN FULL LIVERY; SOON ONE OF THEM BROUGHT US SHERRY. ANOTHER, WHO AS WELL AS LIVERY WORE A PERUKE, WAS ESPECIALLY APPOINTED TO ATTEND US AND LED THE WAY WHENEVER WE LEFT THE SUITE.

AFTER A FEW MINUTES OF CONTEMPLATING THE SCENE, JOE TURNED TO ME AND SAID, "ROSE, THIS IS A HELL OF A LONG WAY FROM EAST BOSTON."

THAT WEEKEND AT WINDSOR WAS ONE OF THE MOST FABULOUS, FASCINATING EXPERIENCES OF MY LIFE. I TOOK MANY DIARY NOTES. THESE ARE EXCERPTS WHICH I HOPE WILL BE INTERESTING TO OTHERS: "AT 8:20 THE FOOTMAN CAME TO ESCORT US TO THE GREEN RECEPTION ROOM. AT 8:30 THE KING AND QUEEN CAME IN AND GREETED EVERYBODY BY SHAKING HANDS. ALL THE LADIES CURTSIED. DINNER WAS ANNOUNCED AND THE KING AND QUEEN WALKED AHEAD ....

*"There were numerous servants in evidence, in full livery;
soon one of them brought us sherry. Another, who as well as
livery wore a peruke [wig], was especially appointed to
attend us and led the way whenever we left the suite . . . At
8:20 the footman came to escort us to the Green Reception
Room. At 8:30 the King and Queen came in . . .*

*I found it very difficult to accustom myself to saying 'Ma'am' when
addressing the Queen and she told me not to bother; putting me at
my ease. She has a very pleasant voice, a beautiful English com-
plexion, great dignity and charm; is simple in manner, stands very
erect and holds herself well and is every inch a queen. . . .*

*I lay in bed thinking [I] must be dreaming that I, Rose Kennedy, a
simple, young matron from Boston, am really here at Windsor
Castle the guest of the Queen and two little Princesses."*

—From Rose Kennedy's account

☙ President Jimmy Carter

Pope John Paul II's Visit to the White House, 1979

In October 1979, when Pope John Paul II made his first papal pilgrimage to the United States, he took the country by storm. Describing himself as a "messenger of brotherhood and peace," the pope traveled to six American cities preaching a message of freedom and human dignity to millions of Americans. *Time* magazine dubbed him "John Paul, Superstar," for the enormous crowds that he drew and the wild enthusiasm they showed for him.

On October 6, President Carter welcomed him to the White House where the two men met privately in the Oval Office for an hour. At the start of the meeting, these two deeply religious men—each at the pinnacle of power in their respective spheres—agreed to speak not as diplomats, but as Christian brothers. Eventually, their discussions turned to world affairs. But first, the President asked the Pope how he handled the adulation; John Paul II, who ministered to the world's 1.1 billion Catholics and stood up to tyrants and dictators around the world with an age-old message of hope, said that he prayed about that more than anything.

President Carter's notes from that historic meeting are shown here.

President Jimmy Carter's notes from his private meeting with Pope John Paul II, October 6, 1979
Although his notes are sketchy, they show that the discussion included particular situations in the Philippines, China, Europe, South Korea, and the Middle East. The White House issued a statement that day stating that during the meeting "the Pope and the President agreed that efforts to advance human rights constitute the compelling idea of our times." *National Archives, Jimmy Carter Presidential Library and Museum, Atlanta, Georgia.*

President Jimmy Carter with Pope John Paul II, photograph by Bill Fitz-Patrick, October 6, 1979
Pope John Paul II was the first pope ever to visit the White House. *National Archives, Jimmy Carter Presidential Library and Museum, Atlanta, Georgia [NLJC-13525.15]*

America on the Move

❧ John C. Frémont

Exploring Expedition to the Rocky Mountains, 1843

"We reached the ford of the Kansas [River] late in the afternoon . . . I had expected to find the river fordable, but it had been swollen by the late rains, and was sweeping by with an angry current, yellow and turbid . . ."

—John Charles Frémont, March 1, 1843

John C. Frémont, photograph from the Mathew Brady Collection, ca. 1860–65

National Archives, Records of the Office of the Chief Signal Officer [111-B-3756]

John C. Frémont's official report on the 1842 expedition he led to the Rocky Mountains reads like a great adventure story. Frémont's father-in-law, Thomas Hart Benton, a powerful senator from Missouri and strong proponent of western expansion, was a major supporter of the expedition, whose purpose was to survey and map the Oregon Trail to the Rocky Mountains. The senator hoped it would encourage Americans to emigrate and develop commerce along the western trails.

The party that included some twenty Creole and Canadian voyageurs and the legendary Kit Carson, started out just west of the Missouri border, crossed the present-day states of Kansas, Nebraska, and Wyoming, and ascended what the men believed to be the highest peak in the Wind River region of the Rockies. Frémont's report provided practical information about the geology, botany, and climate of the West that guided future emigrants along the Oregon Trail; it shattered the misconception of the West as the Great American Desert.

Upon his return home to Washington, DC, Frémont dictated much of the report to his wife, Jessie Benton Frémont, a gifted writer. "The horseback life, the sleep in the open air," she later recalled, "had unfitted Mr. Frémont for the indoor work of writing," and so she helped him. Distilled from Frémont's notes and filtered through the artistic sensibilities of his wife, the report is a practical guide, infused with the romance of the western trail.

"A Report of an Exploration of the Country Lying between the Missouri River and the Rocky Mountains on the Line of the Kansas and Great Platte Rivers," by John Charles Frémont, March 1, 1843, selected pages

These pages recount the party's fording of the Kansas River near present-day Topeka on June 14, 1842, four days after setting out just west of the Missouri border. After riding and driving the animals across, the party used their inflatable rubber boat to ferry their provisions. On the seventh and last trip, Frémont describes how the boat capsized spilling carts, boxes, and barrels into the water. Most were recovered; but almost the entire provision of coffee was lost—a loss that would be often and mournfully remembered.

The first nineteen pages of the report, including these, are in the hand of Jessie Benton Frémont. *National Archives, Records of the Office of the Chief of Engineers*

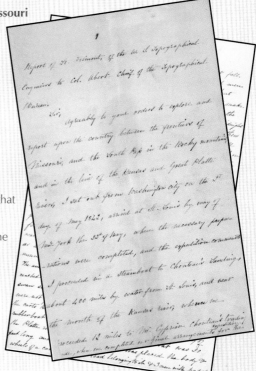

View of the Red Buttes, along the Oregon Trail, photograph by William Henry Jackson, 1870
National Archives, Records of the U.S. Geological Survey, 1839–2001
[57-HS-277]

"*I put upon the boat the remaining two carts with their accompanying loads. The man at the helm was timid in water, and in his alarm capsized the boat. Carts, barrels, boxes and bales, were in a moment floating down the current, but all the men who were on the shore, jumped into the water, without stopping to think if they could swim and almost everything, even heavy articles . . . were recovered . . . but our heaviest loss was a bag of coffee, which contained nearly all our provision. It was a [loss] which none but a traveller in a strange and inhospitable country can appreciate, and often afterwards when excessive toil, and long marching had overcome us with fatigue and weariness, we remembered and mourned over our loss in the Kansas. . . .*"

—From John C. Frémont's report

❧ Laura Ingalls Wilder

A Journey from South Dakota to Missouri, 1894

"The whole country is just full of emigrants, going and coming."

—Laura Ingalls Wilder, 1894

When most people think of Laura Ingalls Wilder, they conjure up a young, fictionalized version of the author—a persona created in *Little House on the Prairie*, and other beloved children's books that portrayed the hardscrabble life of an American pioneer family in the late-nineteenth century. We catch a glimpse of the real Laura Ingalls Wilder as a young wife and mother, in a diary that she kept during the summer of 1894 when she, her husband, Almanzo, and their seven-year-old daughter, Rose, moved from South Dakota to Missouri.

The Wilders' move came after years of hardship in De Smet, South Dakota—drought and crop failure, a case of diphtheria that left Almanzo physically debilitated, the devastating loss of their infant son, and an accident that caused their house to burn down.

Throughout the 650-mile journey that took six weeks, Laura chronicled the weather, the people, and the places they saw. Her diary reflects how her spirits lifted as they moved away from the harshness of the dusty prairie into a lavish landscape of trees and fruit. And it reveals, not just her own journey, but a whole country on the move—trails clogged with covered wagons—hundreds of people leaving heartbreak and disappointment behind, daring to hope for a better life on the road ahead.

ON THE WAY HOME, *The Diary of a Trip from South Dakota to Mansfield, Missouri, in 1894,* by Laura Ingalls Wilder, selected page As she traveled, Laura wrote her diary in pencil in a little five-cent memorandum book. Years later, her daughter Rose edited the diary, added an introductory "setting," and published it in 1962 under the title ON THE WAY HOME—The Diary of a Trip from South Dakota to Mansfield, Missouri, in 1894. This typed manuscript was produced as part of the publication process. *National Archives, Herbert Hoover Presidential Library and Museum, West Branch, Iowa © 1962, 1990 Little House Heritage Trust. Used with permission.*

August 20: Got a good start at 7:30 but the roads are awfully stony. Crops are poor. Everyone tells us they never get rain here when they need it. . . .

August 21: . . . Met a family of emigrants who have spent the last two months traveling in southwest Missouri. They do not like it at all down there . . . We passed another covered wagon stopped by the road, and those folks are on their way to Missouri. The whole country is just full of emigrants, going and coming.

August 29: . . . Parts of Nebraska and Kansas are well enough but Missouri is simply glorious. . . . The sky seems lower here, and it is the softest blue . . . It is a drowsy country that makes you feel wide awake and alive but somehow contented . . . There are masses of blackberries, and seedling peaches and plums and cherries, and luscious-looking fruits ripening in little trees that I don't know, a lavishness of fruit growing wild. It seems to be free for the taking.

—From ON THE WAY HOME by Laura Ingalls Wilder

Laura Ingalls Wilder as a young woman, not dated
Courtesy of Laura Ingalls Wilder Home Association, Mansfield, Missouri

"Rocky Ridge Farm in Mansfield after Almanzo had cleared a good deal of the land," photograph by Laura Ingalls Wilder, ca. 1910
Laura and Almanzo bought land, cleared it, built a house ("We cut and planed and fitted every stick of it ourselves," Laura said), and lived out their long lives on the farm they called Rocky Ridge. *Courtesy of Laura Ingalls Wilder Home Association, Mansfield, Missouri*. Excerpt from: ON THE WAY HOME, The Diary of a Trip from South Dakota to Mansfield, Missouri, in 1894, by Laura Ingalls Wilder

❧Lt. Col. Dwight D. Eisenhower

Transcontinental Motor Convoy, 1919

"In Illinois [the convoy] started on dirt roads, and practically no more pavement was encountered until reaching California."

—Lt. Col. Dwight D. Eisenhower, an observer on the Transcontinental Motor Convoy, November 3, 1919

At the end of World War I, in which vehicles played a vital role, the U.S. War Department wanted to know if the country's roads could handle long-distance emergency movements of motorized army units across the nation. As a test, the Transcontinental Motor Convoy—some 80 military vehicles and 280 officers and enlisted personnel—set out for California from Washington, DC, on July 7, 1919.

In the manner of the wilderness scouts of the nineteenth century, army personnel mounted on Harley-Davidsons instead of horses, would run ahead of the convoy to check out the conditions that lay just ahead. The vehicles broke down, got stuck in dust, quicksand, and mud, and sank when roads and bridges collapsed under them. Sixty-two days after it left Washington, DC, the convoy reached San Francisco. It had covered 3,251 miles, averaging 58 miles a day at an average speed of 6 miles an hour. The official report of the War Department, chronicling the 230 motor accidents of the convoy, concluded that the existing roads in the United States were "absolutely incapable of meeting the present day traffic requirements."

One of the army observers on the convoy was Armored Corps representative, Lt. Col. Dwight D. Eisenhower, a 28-year-old officer grown bored with his peacetime posting at Fort Meade. His summary report is presented here.

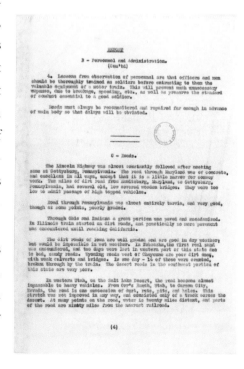

Previous page: Lt. Col.
Dwight D. Eisenhower's
**summary report on the
Transcontinental Motor
Convoy, November 3,
1919, selected page**
The convoy made its way
west via the Lincoln
Highway (now U.S. 30),
passing through some
350 towns. Half of the
distance traveled was
over dirt roads, wheel
paths, desert sands, and
mountain trails. Eisen-
hower later said the roads
they encountered "varied
from average to non-exis-
tent." *National Archives,
Dwight D. Eisenhower
Presidential Library and
Museum, Abilene, Kansas*

Lemonade — gratis.

Lt. Col. Dwight D. Eisenhower, 1919

The experience, which Eisenhower later described as "a genuine adventure" left a
lifelong impression on him. Thirty-seven years later, as President of the United
States, Eisenhower signed into law the Federal-Aid Highway Act of 1956, funding
the National System of Interstate and Defense Highways which established more
than 41,000 miles of superhighway. *National Archives, Dwight D. Eisenhower
Presidential Library and Museum, Abilene, Kansas [NLDDE-62-286-2]*

"Lemonade—gratis," 1919

Although the convoy was intended to be self-sustaining to simulate wartime conditions, this goal was undermined by the barbecues, melon fests, and other offerings
of the hospitable Americans who welcomed the convoy to their towns.

Eisenhower annotated this photograph. *National Archives, Dwight D.
Eisenhower Presidential Library and Museum, Abilene, Kansas [NLDDE-81-17-51]*

❧Crew of *Apollo 8*
A View from Lunar Orbit, 1968

"The vast loneliness up here of the moon is awe inspiring and it makes you realize just what you have back there on Earth. The Earth from here is a grand [oasis] to the big vastness of space."

—Jim Lovell, crew member of the *Apollo 8* spacecraft, December 24, 1968

On December 21, 1968, the three-man crew aboard the *Apollo 8* space-craft—Frank Borman, Jim Lovell, and Bill Anders—lifted off from Cape Kennedy and began a journey that would take them farther away from Earth than anyone had ever gone. Their mission was a crucial step in the Government's program to land a man on the Moon by the end of the 1960s. They were to travel some 240,000 miles from Earth, enter lunar orbit, scout for appropriate landing sites, and prepare the way for future lunar-landing missions.

The flight plan called for the crew to broadcast a public message from lunar orbit on Christmas Eve. The audience was half a billion people around the world. After describing the desolation and bleakness of the lunar land-scape, the astronauts read from an ancient text they had brought with them: "In the beginning, God created the heaven and the earth," Anders began. Each of the three astronauts read in succession the first ten verses from the Book of Genesis, with Frank Borman, commander of the mission, conclud-ing the broadcast, "And from the crew of *Apollo 8*, we close with good night, good luck, a merry Christmas, and God bless all of you—all of you on the good Earth."

Apollo 8 crewmembers, left to right: James A. Lovell, Jr., William A. Anders, and Frank Borman, November 22, 1968
Courtesy of National Aeronautics and Space Administration, Washington, DC

Earthrise, photograph, by Bill Anders, 1968
The crew of *Apollo 8* was armed with still and movie cameras to photograph the Moon; but the most enduring image of their mission is this photograph of their own home, planet Earth.

According to Anders, the astronauts saw the horizon vertically—not horizontally—with the lunar surface to the right. *National Archives, Records of the U.S. Information Agency [306-PSD-68-4049c]*

```
                              NASA-CFD TAPE No. T-01605
                                   (REEL #2)


APOLLO 8 MISSION COMMENTARY,12/24/68,GET 853900,CST 8:31p,274/2

     SC             of what he's seen today.  I know my own
impression is that it's a vast, lonely forbidding type existence,
great expanse of nothing, that looks rather like clouds and
clouds of pumice stone, and it certainly would not appear to be
a very inviting place to live or work.  Jim what have you
thought most about.
     SC             Well, Frank, my thoughts are very similar.
The vast loneliness up here of the moon is awe inspiring and
it makes you realize just what you have back there on Earth.
The Earth from here is a grand ovation to the big vastness
of space.
     SC             Bill, what do you think?
     SC             I think the thing that impressed me the
most was the Lunar's sunrises and sunsets.  These in particular
bring out the stark nature of the terrain and the long shad-
dows really bring out the relief that is here and hard to
see and is very bright -

END OF TAPE.
```

Frank Borman: The moon is a different thing to each one of us. I think that each one of us—each one carries his own impression of what he's seen today. I know my own impression is that it's a vast, lonely forbidding type existence, great expanse of nothing, that looks rather like clouds and clouds of pumice stone, and it certainly would not appear to be a very inviting place to live or work.

Acknowledgments

This book, *Eyewitness—American Originals from the National Archives*, and the exhibit upon which it is based originated in the National Archives, Office for Records Services–Washington, DC. Bringing these eyewitness accounts from the stacks and vaults of the National Archives to our exhibition gallery and to the pages of this book was an agency-wide effort. Marvin Pinkert, Executive Director of the National Archives Experience, guided and oversaw the "Eyewitness" project from inception to completion. Christina Rudy Smith, Director of Exhibits, managed and coordinated all its different elements. Stacey Bredhoff, Senior Curator on the Exhibits Staff, selected the eyewitness accounts and wrote the text describing them. Michael Jackson designed the exhibit; Darlene McClurkin, Senior Researcher on the Exhibits Staff, led the picture and audiovisual research, and did curatorial research for the exhibit and book. Karen Hibbitt and James Zeender were the exhibit registrars; Brian Barth from the Product Development Staff designed the book; and Maureen MacDonald from the same office was the project editor. Tom Nastick, Audiovisual Specialist, edited the audiovisual selections and produced the excerpted presentations; Catherine Farmer, Program Assistant for the National Archives Experience, Bruce Bustard, Jennifer Nichols, Ray Ruskin, and Will Sandoval of the Exhibits Staff, all contributed in countless ways.

The support of the Foundation for the National Archives made the publication of this book possible. Thora Colot, Executive Director; Franck Cordes, Executive Administrator, Stefanie Mathew, Director of Development; Christina Gehring, Publications and Research Manager; and Bruce Banks, Accounting Manager, played key roles in bringing this project to completion.

The eyewitness accounts presented here were drawn from the nationwide holdings of the National Archives, and I am grateful to Sharon Fawcett, Assistant Archivist for Presidential Libraries, and Tom Mills, Assistant Archivist for Regional Records Services, for their cooperation and assistance.

The process of selecting the eyewitness accounts was guided by a large number of archivists inside the National Archives who identified and located records throughout the agency: Greg Bradsher, Rich Boylan, Jane Fitzgerald, Rebecca Livingston, Tim Mulligan, Richard Peuser, Trevor Plante, Constance Potter, James S. Rush, Ken Schlessinger, David Van Tassel, Reginald Washington, and Mitch Yockelson in the Textual Archives Services Division, Washington, DC; Tim Wehrkamp from the Policy and Planning Staff; Les Waffen, Mary Ilario, Holly Reed, Sharon Culley, Nicholas Natanson, and Kate Flaherty in the Special Media Archives Services Division, Washington, DC; Jessica Kratz and Ed Schamel (retired) in the Center for Legislative Archives; Nancy Shader and John Celardo (retired) from the National Archives–Northeast Region (New York City); James McSweeney, Charles Reeves and Mary Evelyn Tomlin from the National Archives–Southeast Region, Atlanta, Georgia; Tim Walch, Spencer Howard, and Jim Detlefesen, at the Herbert Hoover Presidential Library and Museum in West Branch, Iowa; Mark Renovitch at the Franklin D. Roosevelt Presidential Library and Museum in Hyde Park, New York; Ray Geselbracht, Pauline Testerman, Amy Williams, Mark Beveridge, and Randy Sowell at the Harry S. Truman Presidential Library in Independence, Missouri; David Haight, James Leyerzapf, Kathleen Struss, Dennis Medina, and Michelle Kopfer at the Dwight D. Eisenhower Presidential Library and Museum in Abilene, Kansas; Allan Goodrich, Megan Desnoyers, Stephen Plotkin, Susan Wrynn, James Hill, and Maryrose Grossman at the John F. Kennedy Presidential Library and Museum in Boston, Massachusetts; Claudia Anderson, Regina Greenwell, Philip Scott, and Michael MacDonald at the Lyndon B. Johnson Presidential Library and Museum in Austin, Texas; Steve Greene from the Nixon Presidential Materials Staff in College Park, Maryland; Nancy Mirshah from the Gerald R. Ford Presidential Library in Ann Arbor, Michigan; Jay Hakes, Robert Bohanan, James Yancy, David Stanhope, Albert Nason, and Nancy Hassett at the Jimmy Carter Presidential Library and Museum in Atlanta, Georgia; and Warren

Finch, Debbi Carter, Mary Finch, Pat Burchfield, and Amy Day at the George Bush Presidential Library and Museum, in College Station Texas.

We owe a special debt of gratitude to the following historians and writers who graciously agreed to review the exhibit captions. Kenneth Bowling, co-editor, *The Documentary History of the First Federal Congress, 1789–1791*; James Hutson, Chief, Manuscript Division, Library of Congress; Michael Biel, Professor of Communication and Theatre, Morehead State University; Peter Black, Senior Historian, United States Holocaust Memorial Museum; David W. Blight, Class of 1954 Professor of American History, Yale University; Steven J. Dick, Director, NASA History Division; Milton O. Gustafson, retired senior archivist, National Archives; Michael Kauffman, Lincoln assassination author and historian; Ralph E. Luker, civil rights author and historian; Ed Marolda, Senior Historian, Naval Historical Center; John Miller, Professor Emeritus of History, South Dakota State University; and Robert Moore, Historian, Jefferson National Expansion Memorial. These scholars were generous with their time, skill, and expertise, offering important insights and suggestions; we are deeply grateful for their contributions.

Terry Boone, of the Document Conservation Laboratory, led the conservation work on the documents, assisted by Lisa Isbell, Susan Peckham, and Yoonjoo Strumfels. In the Special Media Preservation Laboratory, Amy Young photographed the documents and Steve Puglia, Jeff Reed, and Erin Rhodes of the Digital Laboratory produced the scans of the documents and photographs for this book; Audiovisual Preservation Specialist Charles Mayn provided technical assistance.

Jeff Hartley, Randall Fortson, and Carolyn Gilliam of the National Archives Library fulfilled countless requests for materials.

I would like to thank Susan Cooper, Laura Diachenko, and Miriam Kleiman who have enthusiastically spread the word about "Eyewitness."

The hundreds of people who contributed to "Eyewitness" cannot all be named here. But, wholeheartedly, I thank them all.

MICHAEL J. KURTZ
Assistant Archivist for Records Services—Washington, DC